The Saints of Cornwall

GILBERT H. DOBLE

The Saints of Cornwall

PART TWO

Saints of the Lizard District

Facsimile Reprint by
LLANERCH PUBLISHERS
FELINFACH (1997)

ISBN 1 86143 042 6

Contents

SAINTS OF THE LIZARD DISTRICT

SAINT SITHNEY or SEZNI*

PATRON OF SITHNEY

OF the Celtic saints most nearly connected with Helston, S. Sithney is the only one who is at all widely known. He is not honoured elsewhere in Cornwall,[1] but his cult is found all over Brittany, and a written Life of S. Sezni is in existence.

The Cornish tradition of S. Sithney—the softened Cornish form of Sezni—is soon told. William of Worcester in 1478 tells us that he was buried in Sithney church. Fifty years later Leland read in the Life of S. Breaca then preserved in Breage church that "Breaca came to Cornwall accompanied by many saints, among whom were *Sinninus* the abbot who was at Rome with Patrick, Maruanus the monk, Germochus the king, Elwen, Crewenna, Helena." The churchtown farm at Sithney is called Merther Sithney, *i.e.*, the *martyrium* or chapel of Sithney, a sure sign of an early Celtic foundation; and there appears to be a small statue of the patron saint beneath one of the pinnacles of the tower.

In Brittany, Sezni is the patron of the large coast parish of Guisseny, north-east of Brest. In 1516 Guisseny was called Ploesezny. *Plou* of course simply means *parish*. *Guic* is the Latin *vicus*, and in Léon is very commonly used to denote the churchtown of a parish. It is to be noted that both in Cornwall and in Brittany the consonant before the "n" had been dropped by the seventeenth century. Norden refers to the Cornish parish as "Synny.

* Cornish Saints Series, no. 18 (1928).

1 "The name Sithney occurs in several place-names in other parts of Cornwall. There is a Tresithney in St. Columb [*Tresythny*, 1350] and a Tresinney in Advent near Camelford. Bossiney [Bot-Sithney] occurs at Tintagel. Occasinney in Altarnon is probably connected with the river name of Inney. There is, however, no reason to suppose that S. Sithney had any other church, chapel or well under his patronage in Cornwall beyond the parish-church now bearing his name near Helston," wrote Charles Henderson. The same scholar shows that the name Goldsithney derives from the market or fair transferred thither from Sithney by Robert of Mortain *c.* 1085.

A parish called in records Sythney," and Sithney is still sometimes locally pronounced *Sinny*.[2] In Guisseny church is a fine eighteenth-century statue of the saint, and an earlier one in the porch. At Menez ar Groaz, a mile or so east of the churchtown, is the holy well of S. Sezni, in a lonely spot at the end of a little wood; over the well is a charming medieval statue of Sezni. (It is to be observed that this holy well is on the way to the Peniti Sant Sezni, to be mentioned later).

There was formerly a *minihy* of some note at Guisseny, as Grégoire de Rostrenen, in his dictionary (published in 1732) under the word *Moinerie*, cites as instances of minihys *le minihy Plouguin* and *le minihy Guisseny*. A minihy (*monachia*) means a piece of church land, granted centuries ago to some saint or monastery, and possessing certain privileges, including very often the right of sanctuary. It often bore the name of the saint to whom it had been granted, and a procession is held each year to prevent the bounds of the minihy being forgotten. (So important is this considered, that there is a story that at Minihy-Briac one year when the clergy considered the weather too bad to hold the procession, the cross and the banners went round by themselves!) "A minihy procession, which no doubt was called *Dro sant sezny*, must formerly have existed at Guisseny, for a document (*Compte de fabrique*) of 1616 refers to the *procession et tours Saint-Sény*" (Largillière, *Les Minihys*, p. 197).

There is a Lossefny (Loc-sesny) in Loguivy-Plou-gras, and a Saint-Seny in Kernilis, and a chapel of S. Seznec, which may (J. Loth thinks) be the same as Sezni, in the parish of Plogonnec near Quimper; a Trezeny in the Côtes-du-Nord, and another Guisseny in Bouvron, in the department of Loire-Inférieure—in

[2] Another form of the name is *Sidney*. Sidney is now a very common English name. I think it may have partly owed its popularity to Sidney Godolphin. Now the Godolphins came from the next parish to Sithney, Breage. So the chief city of Australia may, indirectly, owe its name to this Cornish saint. The fame of Sir Philip Sidney, however, has probably most to do with the popularity of the name. There is a place-name *Sidney* in Sussex, but the Sidney family did not take their name from it, as Sir Philip's grandfather, Sir William Sidney, was the first member of the family to acquire land in the south of England (he exchanged lands in York and Lincoln for property in Kent and Sussex in 1539). Their ancestor is said to have been chamberlain to King Henry II, and to have come with him from Anjou (where the cult of Celtic saints is widely spread). Professor Mawer writes to me saying, "The only Sidney that I am aware of as a place-name is one in Cuckfield in Sussex. That is first found in a personal name Wm. *Bysuthenee* in a Subsidy Roll of 1296, and next as *Southney* (place-name) in a Recovery Roll of 1606. This means 'south of the water, OE *éa*' " The name of our saint is *Siduinus* in the register of Bishop Stapeldon (1310), *Sidnius* in that of Bronescombe (1276), *Sydnyny* and *Sidnini* in that of Grandisson (1336 and 1363), *Sidenini* in that of Brantyngham (1392), *Sithnini* in that of Stafford (1403).

the opposite corner of Brittany. The principal focus of the cult of S. Sezni is at Guisseny in Léon. The written legend connects him with Guisseny, and oral traditions about him have persisted there.

The written legend of S. Sezni has been preserved for us by the famous Dominican of Morlaix, Albert Le Grand, whose *Vies des saints de la Bretagne armorique* appeared in 1636. He gives the sources of his Life of S. Sezni—chiefly lections for the feast in the breviaries used in the diocese of Léon, which he has worked over and re-written in his usual way. I shall give a faithful reproduction of this Life, merely noting here that a Breton translation of Albert Le Grand's version, entitled *Buez Sant Sezny*, was printed at Landerneau in 1848. At the end is the name of the translator (?), Marie-Gabrielle Tréguier, with the note: "This Life was made according to the desire of a Tréguier girl of Kervenouen, who asked to have it long ago, hoping that she might have the happiness to beseech the lord S. Sezny to protect before God those who had copied this Life for her. Amen."

The Life of Saint Sezni

Bishop, Confessor and Patron of the Parish of Guic-Sezni in Léon, September 19[3]

I. In the time when Pope Innocent I occupied the holy apostolic see, and Arcadius and Honorius were emperors, King Grallon reigning in Armorican Britain, in the year of grace 402, S. Sezni was born in the island of Yrlande (Ireland) or Hybernia, in the province now called *Ultonia* (Ulster) and at that time known as *Ostrinct*.[4] His father was called *Ernut*,[5] and his mother *Wingella*, who, before their child was born, had a vision which seemed to foretell that he whom she was shortly to give to the world would be a light to enlighten many and lead them to eternal salvation. For lying in bed one night with her face turned to the heavens, she saw the firmament strewn with stars, one of which, more brilliant than the others, seemed to fall into her mouth and be swallowed by her. When the child was born, he was baptized, and called Sezni; and, as soon as he could speak distinctly, he was sent to school, where he profited greatly in his studies and yet more in the cultivation of virtue. Returning to his family, he resolved to leave the world, and to retire to an

[3] The Bollandists observe that the feast of S. Sezni is kept at Guisseny with great solemnity on March 6. Colgan suggests that September 19 might be the feast of his translation.

[4] In some notes Fr Paul Grosjean, S.J., Bollandist, very kindly sent me, he writes, "I have no suggestion to offer as to the connotation of *Ostrinct*, except that it looks rather impossible Irish."

[5] Fr Grosjean remarks "Duine thinks, on Colgan's authority, it seems, that *Ernan* and *Fingella* are better forms of the names of the saint's parents. To put those names in a less latinized shape, they would be something like *Ernan* (modernized, *Earnan*) and *Findgel* (modernized, *Fionnghéal*), both not uncommon personal names."

island off the coast, then called *Clarac*, where he remained till he was twenty-three years old, when he was inspired by God to go to Rome, to serve him in an occasion which was soon to arise.

II. He arrived at Rome in the year 425, in the reign of Valentinian, and began to frequent the schools for the study of Holy Scripture, and contracted a friendship with S. Patrick, who, already consecrated bishop, and destined to convert all the remaining pagans in Hybernia, knowing the sanctity and ability of S. Sezni, presented him to Pope S. Celestine I, who consecrated him bishop and joined him to S. Patrick to help him in his campaign for the conquest of souls. The two saints, having received their apostolic mission, together with the pope's blessing, bearing many fine relics and other presents, crossed to Great Britain and from there to Hybernia, where St. Patrick, who was well received by the people, sent S. Sezni to a canton of the island then called *Warrham*, giving him some priests and monks to assist him in his work.

Having arrived at the country assigned to him, he set to work to evangelize these islanders with great zeal, and in a short time converted so many of them that they built a church, and afterwards monastic buildings to lodge him and his company; and so many people were converted every day that, to assist him in instructing them, and in catechizing, baptizing and ministering the sacraments, he was obliged to ordain still more priests. His mission having proved so successful, he informed S. Patrick, and also Pope S. Sixtus III (the successor of S. Celestine), who made his monastery into a bishopric, and appointed him the first bishop. The church of his monastery having thus become a cathedral, he built another monastery larger than the first, where he received a great number of young men and instructed them in virtuous living, in order to appoint them to the cures and benefices of his diocese, and to employ them in preaching and in the other duties of their office. He was well rooted in humility, patient in adversities, untiring in the work of preaching and the conversion of souls, chaste, a lover of poverty, austere in his manner of life, gentle to all, assiduous in prayer and contemplation, preaching more by example than by word; he never drank wine nor intoxicating drink, and for clothing contented himself with the skins of beasts, without using linen or wool except for his pontifical ornaments.

III. God sanctioned his mission and preaching by an infinite number of miracles, by which he sealed the truth of his doctrine. The lamps of the church being one day extinguished, he re-kindled a fire by his prayers, and carried live coals in his hands without burning himself. The holy hermit Rhodon came to visit him one winter day when it was very cold: S. Sezni conducted him to the hospice, put fagots in the fireplace, and, not finding any fire to kindle them with, fell to prayer, and the fire enkindled of itself. Having been asked to eat with a nobleman named *Gerran*, he raised to life one of his servants who had been recently strangled by the wolves in the forest close by. He went to visit the prince of this country, whom he had converted, and found the princess *Onegia* ill in bed, and so off her feed that she could not eat anything. The saint, after speaking a few words to edification, asked her if there was anything she fancied. The patient replied that she would like some blackberries, and the saint said "Madam, set your mind at rest; I will get you some;" and soon afterwards he obtained some by his prayers and gave them to her, and as soon as she had eaten them she was cured.

IV. S. Patrick came to see him in his monastery one day, and the wine (which is very rare in that country) gave out; S. Sezni made the sign of the cross over some jars of water which were in his monastery, and the water was changed into wine, which lasted the whole three days S. Patrick stayed there. He raised to life seven men who had been killed by robbers and their bodies thrown into a pond. A poor man having by mistake killed a fine horse belonging to his master, he was, by the latter's command, thrown into prison and his feet put in irons: S. Sezni went to see this lord and asked him to set his poor prisoner at liberty; and on his refusal, he raised the horse to life and returned it to him, and so set the prisoner free. Two Hybernian princes having fallen out, all attempts at reconciliation failing, they resolved to go to war, and assembled their armies to fight with each other: S. Sezni visited them and exhorted them to peace, but seeing they obstinately resolved to fight, retired, saying that as he himself could do nothing God would take the matter into his own hands. The two armies regarded each other, but when they attempted to engage in combat they found all their efforts in vain, by reason of a great beam which separated them from one another each time they advanced, so that finally, seeing that they were miraculously prevented from fighting, they came to an agreement, thanking God and S. Sezni for having averted so great a slaughter.

V. S. Sezni having confirmed the Hybernians in the faith and doctrine of Christ, wishing to live the rest of his life in repose, was inspired by God to cross the sea, and to go to Armorican Britain, taking with him a good number of his religious, which he did. Embarking with seventy of his disciples, he was carried by a favourable wind to the coast of Léon, to a haven named *Poulluhen*, in the parish of *Kerloüan*, where they landed in the year 477, the same year that the Franks or French crossed the Rhine to enter Gaul, towards the end of the reign of Hoel the Great, king of Brittany. S. Sezni settled near this port, and built there a little hermitage for himself and his companions, which is still to be seen and is called *Peneti Sant Sezni*. From there he moved to the place where now stands the parish-church of *Guic-Sezni*, built there a monastery, and there lived in great holiness, with his religious, till he reached the advanced age of 127, when God called him to himself, in the year 529, to the great regret of all the inhabitants of Léon. His body was buried in his monastery, under the high altar, where the vault of his tomb is still seen. God worked so many miracles at his intercession after his decease that a fleet of Hybernians, having anchored in the port of *Poulluhen*, carried off his body and bore it to his bishopric, from which with great difficulty a few relics have been recovered and are reverently preserved in the said church of Guic-Sezni.

This life has been compiled by us from ancient manuscript legendaries of the cathedral church of Léon and the collegiate church of Notre-Dame-du-Folgoüet, and from an ancient manuscript book kept in the parish church of Guic-Sezni, and from the manuscript memoirs of the noble and discreet Messire Yves le Grand, canon of Léon; the ancient breviaries of Léon and Cornouaille celebrate his festival with nine lessons on September 19, although his feast is kept on March 6 in the parish of Guic-Sezni.

Now everyone familiar with the delightful but uncritical work of Albert Le Grand will recognize at once the characteristics of his method. Such are his attempts at exact chronology (all his

Lives abound with dates, although real history can hardly supply us with a single certain date for the history of Brittany during the early period), his anachronisms (invariably he supposes that Brittany in the sixth century was governed exactly like the duchy of feudal times, and his picture of Sezni's "diocese" with its "benefices" reminds one of Caxton's story of S. Augustine of Canterbury's relations with the curate of Compton in Oxfordshire who "cursed" for his tithes), and his picturesque filling in of the character and careers of persons of whom little or nothing in reality was known with details drawn from his own imagination.

At the same time there is no doubt that Albert Le Grand found the main outlines of his Life of S. Sezni in the authorities to whom he refers. But, as the Bollandists point out in their *Acta Sanctorum* for March 6 (pp. 428, 429), the Life of S. Sezni which Albert Le Grand found in the liturgical books of the diocese of Léon is (with the exception of the last section) simply an abridgement of the Life of another Irish saint, S. Ciarán of Saighir,[6] a saint identified in the middle ages with the Cornish S. Keverne or S. Piran. In a Life of S. Ciarán printed by the Bollandists in the same volume of the *Acta Sanctorum* (March 5, pp. 392 *seq.*), and which they say is taken from a manuscript formerly in the Irish college of the Jesuits at Salamanca,[7] the same story of the mother's dream that a star fell into her mouth is related. A Kilkenny manuscript[8] says he was educated "in the island of *Clera.*" Ciarán goes to Rome, where he is consecrated bishop. He returns to Ireland and settles at Saighir, near the fountain of *Fuaran*,[9] spelt by Capgrave *Waran* (hence Albert Le Grand's *Warrham*). S. Patrick comes to Munster and baptizes the king Aengus. By accident Patrick's horse is killed by a man of Ossory, who is

[6] Often called *Ciarán the Elder* to distinguish him from Ciarán of Cluain (Clonmacnoise). *Saighir* = Seirkieran.

[7] See the Bollandist *Bibliotheca Hagiographica Latina*, 4658.

[8] Now in Marsh's Library, Dublin. See *Analecta Bollandiana*, 1928, p. 110. The text is in Plummer's *Vitae Sanctorum Hiberniae*, vol. i.

[9] "*Fuaran* means 'the little cold (fountain)', and is not uncommon as the name of a well. The only thing known about this one seems to be that it was at or near Seirkieran. There is a lovely stanza on a fountain of the same name in the Tripartite Life of St Patrick" (Fr Grosjean). The reference is to the following passage: "Then it was that Patrick made the well which is called Uaran-garad, and he loved this water very much, ut ipse dixit (=as he said himself):

Uaran-gar—
O well! which I have loved, which loved me;
Alas! my cry, O dear God!
That my drink is not from the pure well."

brought in chains to the king to be punished. Ciarán is asked to intercede for him, but does so in vain, and finally has to buy his release with a present of gold, which later vanishes into thin air, to the king's chagrin. One April, Ciarán heals the queen of Munster, Ethne, of a languor brought on by an unlawful passion for another king: she says that nothing but a dish of blackberries can save her from death, and Ciarán gives her a branch covered with ripe blackberries, which he had picked the previous autumn, wrapped in a veil. Next we hear that the kings of Tara and Munster go to war, but a battle is prevented by a thick forest and flooded river miraculously appearing between the two armies.

The name *Geran* seems to be taken from Capgrave's Life of S. Ciarán, though the story is different. The boy eaten by wolves appears in another part of the Life of Ciarán. The Easter fire at the abbey of Ross Bennchor, which should have been kept burning throughout the year, was extinguished by a boy out of mischief, but miraculously rekindled by Ciarán. There follows the story of how S. Ruadhan, abbot of Lothra, comes to visit S. Ciarán at Saighir, but unfortunately there is no fire for the guests to warm themselves. Ciarán blesses a stone, which bursts into flame and is carried in the man of God's hands to Ruadhan. A brother upsets the milk, but at Ciarán's prayers the jar is found full of excellent milk. King Aengus of Munster has seven skilled harpers, who play before him and sing to him sweetly the deeds of heroes. The harpers passing through the parish (*plebs*) of Muscraige Tíre in Munster (E. & W. Muskerry, in Co. Cork) are slain by their enemies, who conceal their bodies in a certain pond in the wilderness and hang up their harps on a tree on the bank of the pond. The king cannot imagine what has become of them, but S. Ciarán informs him. The saint then proceeds to the pond and fasts there for a day. The pond then dries up and the harpers come to life, after being a month in the water, pick up their harps, and sing sweet songs to the people before the king and the bishop. The pond has ever since been dry, but is still called *Loch na gCruitireadh*, *i.e.*, the Harpers' Pool. S. Ciarán all his life abstained from the use of soft clothing and intoxicating drinks. He lived 300 years, which Albert Le Grand prudently reduces to 127.

It is perfectly clear, then, that the traditional Life of S. Sezni in Brittany is copied from the Irish Life of S. Ciarán. The only question is why two saints with names so different have been confused. The Bollandists point out that a saint named *Serenicus*, abbot of *Sagium* (Séez) is venerated in Normandy on May 7, and suggest that the Bretons, knowing nothing about S. Sezni, surmised that Seznaeus and Serenicus were the same, that Sagium was Saighir, and that their saint must be the well known saint of Saighir. They (the Bollandists) wisely conclude that "the only certain thing we know about S. Sezni is the existence of his cult; who he was, where he came from, and what he did, are all a mystery."

The Life of S. Sezni thus tells us nothing whatever about him; it is the Life of an entirely different saint. It is not probable even that Sezni was an Irish saint, as Sezni is a British name.[10] True, Leland tells us that "Sinninus the Abbot" was "at Rome with Patrick" and was among the Irish band that came over with Breaca, but it is probable that the Breton legends used by Albert Le Grand had been brought over to Cornwall by the sixteenth century and acclimatized here.

But the last section of Albert Le Grand's Life does contain several points of real interest. We are to notice that it says that S. Sezni's first settlement in Brittany was, not at Guisseny, but in the adjoining parish of Kerlouan. In the same parish of Kerlouan, on the road to Guisseny, is a hamlet called Treisseni. The large number of place-names in these two parishes containing the name of Sezni is evidence of a long stay of the saint in this neighbourhood. Kerlouan is probably not a very ancient parish; it is clearly a fragment of the huge parish of Guisseny. The fact that the original seat of the cult of S. Sezni is not at the church-town of Guisseny is important; Largillière notes many similar cases in ancient Breton parishes (cf. *Les Saints*, pp. 55, 56, etc.).

Secondly, we learn from Albert Le Grand's Life that Guisseny could not claim the body of S. Sezni. Evidently he did not die there (the story of the Irish fleet carrying it off is of course an invention). Now William of Worcester says that Sithney church

10 "S. Sezny a un nom brittonique" (Largillière, *Les Saints*, p. 129). A bishop called S. Sedna or Sidonius is found in c. iv of the 2nd Vita Sti Senani published in the Bollandist *Acta Sanctorum* (See my *Saint Senan*). A. S. Sedna or Sethna or Setne, was the successor of S. Carthach as bishop at Saighir: see *Vita Sti Moluae*, c. 35, vol. ii, p. 218, of Plummer's *Vitae Sanctorum Hiberniae*. The father of S. Maedoc of Ferns was a Connaught man called Sethna or Sethneus (*ib.*, p. 141). The father of S. Comgall, abbot of Bennchor, was also called Sethna or Setneus (*ib.*, p. 3), and a Setny or Secny appears in the 1st Life of S. Brendan c. 102 (*ib.* i, p. 150).

contained the tomb of the patron saint. Can it be that he really did die and was buried in Cornwall?

§

Every student of Brittany knows the writings of Émile Souvestre. In his *Derniers Bretons*, published in 1836, he describes a visit to Guisseny, and gives some legends about the patron saint he heard from an old peasant there. On the sands he saw the cross of S. Sezni, which, though only three feet high, was never, he heard, covered by the sea. This was because it had been erected by S. Sezni himself when he landed there on his arrival in Brittany. The peasant told him that, after landing, he asked hospitality from a rich man in the neighbourhood, who churlishly refused. To protect himself from the weather, Sezni proceeded to build himself a chapel, which he completed in a single night, for the stones came of their own accord and placed themselves in the wall, like sheep entering their fold. When he had finished, the saint threw his hammer into the middle of a field belonging to the rich man. Next day he knocked once more at the door of the latter's farmhouse. "What do you want?" said the owner, "I have already told you that I won't have you in my house." "I only want you to come and cut your corn, which is tall and ripe, so that I may recover my hammer which I have thrown into the middle of your field by the edge of the sea." The rich man thought the stranger was demented, as it was winter and the corn had hardly begun to germinate. "You are laughing at me," he said. "I am not," replied the saint; "come with me, and you shall see if I lie." The farmer followed Sezni, and on arriving at the shore was dumbfounded to see his field covered with ripe corn, while all around the rest of the ground was black and without sign of so much as a blade. Moved to repentance, he fell at the saint's feet and entreated his forgiveness, and was converted, with all his house, to the Catholic faith.

Later, Sezni filled Armorica with the tale of his miracles. One day when he was alone in his cell, God the Father revealed to him that he intended to make him the patron saint of girls. "Ah! not so, Lord, I beseech thee," said Sezni, in alarm. "There is nothing worse than women on this earth, except the Devil. They will be for ever plaguing me to get them husbands and fine clothes, and I shall never have a moment's peace." "Well then," said the Almighty, "how about mad dogs?" "Oh, I don't so much mind about mad dogs," answered Sezni, "I'd rather have mad dogs than women any day." And so the well of S. Sezni flows among the sandhills by the shore, and sick dogs from all the country round are taken there to drink the water to which the saint has communicated the power to heal them (*Derniers Bretons, 3me partie*, c. 3. (People without a sense of humour may need a reminder that the Bretons have a very keen sense of humour, and that this story is not to be taken too seriously).

The following Legend of S. Seny was communicated to the abbé Duine by a nun from Guisseny (see *Revue des Traditions Populaires*, vol. xviii, 1903, pp. 274, 275. My friend M. Le Guennec kindly copied the extracts for me).

I. The Church of S. Seny

S. Seny was born in England. To reach Brittany he crossed the sea in a trough. "Grant me, Lord," he said, "the grace to cast anchor in the place where I am to build my church." Now it came to pass that he cast anchor in a field of flax newly sown. "Give me this field," he said to the farmer. "Alas!" he replied, "I have only just sown it." "That's nothing," returned the saint, beloved of God. And he built his church.

II. S. Seny and His Geese

S. Seny had some geese, and by selling their eggs he got enough money to build his church. But one day a robber stole one of his geese. The saint set out to find the rogue, and said to him, "My friend, give me back my bird." "I haven't seen it," said the man. This lie was answered by God himself working a great miracle, for the goose, which was being roasted in the pot, cried out, "Here I am!" "So powerful shall my malediction on thee be," said S. Seny, "that a priest shall never be found in the family of Bervas, whose name thou bearest." And no Bervas has ever been ordained priest.

III. The Vengeance of S. Seny

S. Seny had a fountain and a beautiful statue. The faithful brought innumerable presents to this statue—rich robes to dress it in, silver crosses, golden hearts and pretty rosaries. But robbers carried them all away. The sacristan, seeing this, said to the saint, "Aren't you ashamed, Seny? You let them strip you as if you were an infant! Do you think that does you credit? You make me blush. If this continues, I give you up." The saint heard these reproaches, and said nothing; but when the sacristan returned next morning, he saw his hand gripping a robber, who screamed and struggled in vain. "That's right, Seny!" said the sacristan, "that's right, my beloved saint. After this, people will have confidence in you."

The abundance of Guisseny folk-lore about the patron saint shows the important place S. Sezni holds in the imagination of the people of that parish. But the true story of his life, as I have said, has been long forgotten. I hope parishioners of Sithney reading these lines will not get a false idea of their patron saint. He was an enthusiastic missionary, who did a great work for Christ in his day. As I said in my article on the Cornish saints in *Tre, Pol and Pen* (1928): "We must not conclude from the childish and often intentionally comic legends which popular imagination has since woven around them, that the men who gave their names to our Cornish parishes were idiots or eccentrics. They were saints and heroes, 'holding forth the word of life in the midst of a crooked and perverse generation among whom they shone as lights in the world' (Phil. 2: 15). They set a high standard of holiness and self-denial amidst violence and unbridled passion. They were patriots, keeping alive the national aspirations of a race exposed to the attacks of cruel and powerful enemies. They were scholars, preserving literature and learning when civilization had almost perished."

An article on the parish of Guisseny was printed a few years ago in the *Bulletin d'histoire et d'archéologie* of the diocese of Quimper. It was written by M. Jourdan de La Passardière and Canon Uguen after an examination of the archives of the parish. They tell us of a tradition in the parish to the effect that when the Irish carried off the relics of S. Sezni (see above) the bells of the church sounded by themselves. The Irish, pursued by the inhabitants, in their haste dropped an arm-bone, which has since been carefully preserved, and is now kept in a reliquary of ebony and silver dating from the eighteenth century. Another tradition adds that S. Brevalaire was the companion of S. Sezni. They drew lots who should settle at Kerlouan. Brevalaire won, and became the patron of Kerlouan. "Well," said Sezni, "I will go wherever my hammer falls." He threw it into the air and it fell two kilometres away, in a field of flax then in flower. Next day the flax was ready to be cut. It was then he built the church of Guisseny.

The tower of Guisseny church was rebuilt in 1700; it is a copy of Plou-daniel. The church itself was rebuilt in 1721, except the north and south porches. There is a fine eighteenth-century statue of S. Sezni in painted wood, north of the high altar (the statue of the patron saint always occupies this position in Breton churches), an older statue in the north porch, and a third in the chapel in the churchyard. The Pardon is on the third Sunday in September. The chief people in the parish have always been glad to gain, by making a generous offering to the church, the privilege of carrying the relics of "Monsieur Saint Sezni" in the Pardon procession. There is a Breton ballad of S. Sezni printed in the 1837 edition of Albert Le Grand.

Before the Revolution there were chapels of the following Celtic saints in the parish (including the *trève* or sub-parish of Saint-Fregan): S. Tujan, Tudan or Tuzan, S. Gildas or Veltas, S. Yves and S. Guénolé. There was a chapel at a place called the Hellez, which is interesting in view of the nearness of Sithney to Helston (Helles-ton). There is a statue of a female martyr, S. Haude, in Guisseny church.

Among the plays of the distinguished French, or rather Breton, dramatist Tanguy Malmanche is one entitled *Les Païens*, in which the scene is laid at Guisseny. A shipwrecked Cornish sailor escapes from the waves, and when asked who he is and where he comes from, astonishes his interlocutor by replying "Sydney [Sithney] is my parish, and Cornwall is my bishopric" (Brittany is divided, not into *counties*, but into *bishoprics*). The fact of these two maritime parishes opposite each other on the Cornish and Breton sides of the English Channel having the same patron saint is most significant. At present the key to the riddle is lost, but that does not make it any the less interesting. We must patiently study everything that may throw more light on this fascinating subject, the history of Celtic Cornwall.

SAINT CONSTANTINE*

PATRON OF CONSTANTINE

THE name Constantine is found in two places in Cornwall—on the shores of Constantine Bay near Padstow, and on the banks of the Helford River in south-west Cornwall.

Constantine Bay takes its name from the ruined church of S. Constantine, on the sand hills in St Merryn parish, near Trevose Head. This part of the parish of St Merryn was formerly a separate district or sub-parish—what in Brittany is called a *trève*. The people who lived in this district claimed that they were "*parishioners* of the chapel of S. Constantine," which had "its parish and parishioners of its own, within the limits of the parish of St Merryn." We find from a very interesting document in the Register of Bishop Brantingham, dated 17 May 1390, that, among other privileges, the "parishioners" of St Constantine were accustomed to have Mass, with blessing of holy bread and holy water, in their chapel every Wednesday and Friday. The owner of the land, Mr Penrose Williams, some years ago discovered in a hedge in the vicinity of the chapel a stone which proves to be one half of a portable altar of Cataclewse stone which had five crosses on it, and which may be the very altar stone used on these occasions. Whether it may perhaps even be the altar of S. Constantine himself is a question for experts to decide. I think it is more probably medieval.

The church was rebuilt in 1390, with a chancel, nave, aisle and tower. In 1568 Constantine was still regarded as a sub-parish, since a deed of that year, discovered by Mr Henderson, describes Treyarnon as "lying in Constenton in the parish of St Merryn." During the century that followed the chapel was abandoned, perhaps owing to the site being rendered difficult of access in winter because the sands choked the bed of the stream and converted the neighbourhood into a marsh.[1] It had a very

*Cornish Saints Series, no. 26 (1930). First printed in the *Truro Diocesan Gazette*, October 1930, being an address given at S. Constantine's Well in St Merryn parish at the diocesan pilgrimage on August 28 in the same year.

[1] Mr Penrose Williams tells me he thinks that "the church was twice destroyed by sand-storms, at least I infer that from the fact that every section of the ground there, and elsewhere about the golf-links, shows two layers of clean sand with a ground surface between. The later (thirteenth-century) church undoubtedly fell in a storm: I have this summer found further remains—portions of a window and string course, among a mass of broken slate and mortar to the north-east, suggesting a south-westerly gale."

beautiful font of Cataclewse stone, which is now in the parish church, whose own font has gone to Maker church. In 1814, we learn from Lysons' *Magna Britannia*, "some broken arches and pillars, of Cataclewse, and a considerable part of the tower" were still standing, and "a richly ornamented aisle is said to have been standing till about 1780." After the chapel ceased to be used for worship, part of it was used as an almshouse. The foundations of the walls can still be seen in the south aisle.[2]

Although the chapel was no longer used, the feast of the patron saint was still observed, as we find from an interesting passage in Lysons: "The Festival of St. Constantine (March 9) was, till very lately, kept at St Merran by an annual hurling match, on which occasion the owner of Harlyn had, from time immemorial, supplied the silver ball. We are informed from good authority that a shepherd's family, of the name of Edwards, held one of the cottages in Constantine for many generations under the owner of Harlyn, by the annual render of a Cornish Pie, made of limpets, raisins, and sweet herbs, at the feast of St Constantine."

Near the ruins of the chapel, 70 yards northward, on the edge of the little stream that drains the valley, is a holy well.[3] Hals saw it in the seventeenth century and described it as follows: "Near this church is yet extant St Constantine's well, strong built of stone and arched over; on the inner part hereof are places or seats for people to sit and wash themselves in the streams thereof; the consequence of which facts, if the inhabitants may be credited, is not only very refreshing and salubrious, but, if it be dry weather, immediately showers of rain will follow."

This belief (which has inspired the story invented or recorded by Hunt in his *Popular Romances of the West of England*, pp. 287-288) is particularly interesting, as it is found in connection with one of the most famous wells in the world—the fountain of Baranton in the forest of Brocéliande in Brittany, of which so many legends are told. "If hunters come to the fountain of Barenton in time of great heat," wrote Wace in the twelfth century," and draw water with their horns and pour it out on the *perron*, rain will fall immediately." The neighbouring parishes

[2] "The church of St Constantine being in part converted now to a dwelling house for poor people," says Hals.

[3] I need hardly say that the statement that the well is mentioned in Domesday Book is without foundation.

in the forest used to go in procession in time of drought to the fountain, with cross and banners, and sprinkle its water with the staff of the cross, in order to obtain rain, and did this as late as 1835.

The well of S. Constantine was overwhelmed in the sand in the eighteenth century and buried eight feet deep. In 1911 Mr Penrose Williams excavated it and found it exactly as Hals described it, except that the roof had partly been destroyed.[4] There is a stone seat on either side, about a foot high, 16 inches wide, and 3 feet long, running along each side wall. At one end is the well, the water of which escapes down a gully in the floor between the seats. When unearthed, this gully was floored with an oak trough. "The side walls gradually curve inward and would meet at a point about seven feet from the floor." Mr Williams completely uncovered the well in 1923, and protected it with a temporary roof. He thinks that it originally stood on the banks of a little estuary, which would account for the position of the church on this otherwise unlikely spot.[5]

We have seen that this ancient chapel and well bore the name of S. Constantine. They stood on land which once belonged to the monks of S. Petroc, and in the kalendar of the priory church of Bodmin William of Worcester, who visited Bodmin in September 1478, found "Saint Constantine, King and Martyr" honoured on March 9.

In West Cornwall there is a large parish called Constantine where the feast is at the beginning of March.[6] In Domesday we find, among "those holding lands in Cornwall," a group entitled "the churches of certain saints." In every case these are especially important churches, the sites of the chief monasteries in Cornwall in Celtic times, and most of them continued as collegiate churches

[4] See his reports in *Proceedings of the Society of Antiquaries* for 1912, and in the *Journal of the Royal Institution of Cornwall*, 1924.

[5] The neighbourhood, now so thinly inhabited, was a centre of population in very early times. "In 1866 two beautiful gold lunulae together with a flat bronze celt were found in a barrow on the cliff near Harlyn House. These lunulae and celt belong to the early Bronze Age, dating before 1000 B.C. They may be seen at the County Museum, Truro. In 1900 a prehistoric burial-ground was discovered at Harlyn Bay. The interments were of what is known as the 'contracted' or 'crouched' type, the cists being of slate. This cemetery is believed to be of the Early Iron Age, with an approximate date of the third century B.C. Some ornaments were found in the cists, including a pair of bronze fibulae and bracelets of bronze and Kimmeridge shale. These may also be seen in the County Museum, Truro" (Note kindly sent me by Mr George Penrose, curator of the Museum).

[6] Nicholas Roscarrock, an Elizabethan writer, gives March 9 as the feast at Constantine in Kerrier, and adds "The inhabitants saye that they have by Tradition that he was King of that Countrey."

through the middle ages. Last on the list comes "Sanctus Constantinus."[7] Mr Henderson discovered that Constantine, though north of the Helford River, formed part of the Meneage—the Monk's Land.[8]

The church of Milton Abbot in Devon, on the Tamar, is also dedicated to S. Constantine. He was, too, patron of chapels in the parishes of Illogan in Cornwall and Dunsford in Devon (on the Teign, near Exeter), licensed by the bishop of Exeter in 1445 and 1421 respectively. We note that all these places are on the sea or close to tidal rivers, which is what we should expect. The Celtic saints travelled usually by water.

Who was Constantine? People who have tried to give an answer to this question have often found themselves involved in the same difficulties as would a person who tried to combine in one biography the lives of all the men called Smith who have lived in England in the last 300 years, including all the Smiths who were hanged for murder and all the Smiths who became bishops. In romanized Britain, after it had become Christian, the name of the first Christian emperor came to be a favourite name, and there were almost as many Constantines in the different kingdoms of the Britons as in the empire of Byzantium.

The Cornish and Welsh Traditions

It was a favourite name in particular with the royal family of Dumnonia. The prince of Dumnonia in Gildas's time bore this name. He calls him "Constantine, the tyrannical whelp of the unclean lioness of Damnonia," who "this same year, after taking a dreadful oath (whereby he bound himelf first before God . . . then called all the saints, and Mother of God, to witness,

[7] Mr Henderson tells me that "The Churchtown lands of Constantine were known, as late as 1574, by their ancient name of *Logstenton* or *Langostentin* (=The Lan or Monastery of Constantine). The name is no longer known. There is evidence to show that the half hide of land mentioned in Domesday as having been the endowment of S. Constantine's church was identical with the later manor of Polwheveral. This includes the Churchtown, Trebarva, Bossahan and Polwheveral, *i.e.* the long ridge of land lying between the head-streams of Polwheveral Creek. This is mostly land of excellent quality, showing that the *Lan* was established in the most fertile spot in the district."

[8] A deed, dated at Penscawen in St Enoder in 1509, speaks of Trevany as being "in Constantine in Meneke." Mr Henderson wishes me however to state that too much must not be made of this reference in a 16th-century deed, which may be a mistake. Confirmatory evidence is at present lacking. [Canon Doble said little about the Kerrier Constantine in this study because of the then forthcoming publication of Henderson's history of that parish: it was published in 1937 by the Royal Institution of Cornwall, *A History of the Parish of Constantine*.—*Ed.*]

that he would not contrive any deceit against his countrymen) he nevertheless, in the habit of an abbot amid the sacred altars, did with sword and javelin, . . . wound and tear, even in the bosoms of their temporal mother, and of the Church their spiritual mother, two royal youths, with their two attendants,"[9] after having "for many years before stained himself with the abomination of many adulteries."

Now I should like to point out that there is not the smallest evidence that the Constantine of Gildas is the S. Constantine whom we find honoured in five parishes of Devon and Cornwall, as some persons (forgetful of the fact that Constantine was a very common name at that time) have rashly assumed. The Constantine we have just heard described may or may not have been in reality as bad as Gildas says, and he may or may not have been converted in later life; but it hardly seems possible that he could be the Constantine who figures so largely in Celtic hagiography and in the toponymy of Devon and Cornwall, who must have lived at a much later date, when Dumnonia had shrunk greatly in area.

Gildas, then, can tell us nothing about S. Constantine, except that it is a likely name for a prince in these parts to bear. The only Cornish tradition about Constantine is the story in the *Vita Petroci*, which must have been suggested to the author of that Life by the fact that there was an important chapel of Constantine near Padstow.

> On a certain day when the servant of God was praying alone in a place where he had been accustomed to pray, he saw a stag appear in the distance, fleeing towards him as hard as it could go, pursued by the huntsmen of Constantine, a rich man, with hallooing and barking of dogs. The servant of God, moved with kindly feeling, protected it from being hurt. The stag was being followed by the chieftain himself, to whom his soldiers, fearing to touch it while under the protection of the man of God, reported the matter in due order. Full of fury, Constantine would have struck the servant of God with his sword, but was suddenly smitten with paralysis, and became unable to move hand or foot, until he besought pardon and

[9] This is Dr Giles's translation, but Mr Wade-Evans considers it "very loose, and inaccurate in one particular." He would render the passage as follows—" making his oath first to God and secondly to the choirs of saints, and those who follow them in reliance upon the Mother (the Church)."

(at the petition of his soldiers) the saint released him by his pious prayers. After freeing him, he taught him and his nineteen soldiers the Christian faith, and made them gentle and kind instead of fierce tyrants, and worshippers of Christ instead of pagans.

It is clearly a pure legend, of the kind that floated about in the literature of the middle ages for any hagiographer to adopt to suit his needs, since exactly similar stories are found in the Lives of S. Neot, S. Kea and S. Brioc, to say nothing of S. Giles and other non-Celtic saints. But we may learn one thing from it, and that is that in the early middle ages there was a tradition in Cornwall of a chieftain named Constantine converted by a saint. In the sixteenth century Leland had heard of a "pious and liberal prince of Cornwall" named Constantine who helped S. Petroc build his monastery.[10]

But Welsh and Irish traditions also speak of a Cornish king named Constantine, who became a monk. Rhigyfarch in his Life of S. David, written about 1090, says that "when therefore the report of holy David's name was heard, kings and princes of this world abandon their kingdoms and seek his monastery. Hence it was that Constantine, king of the Cornishmen, abandoned his kingdom and bent the neck of his pride, untamed before, in humble obedience in the monastery of this father. And when he had followed this mode of life for a long time in faithful service, he at length founded a monastery in another far-off country" (which Rhigyfarch prudently avoids naming). This clearly is not Gildas's Constantine. He is the "King of the Cornishmen," that is, of a kingdom which was only a small fraction of the Dumnonia of Gildas's day, and he must have been a comparatively young man when he began his career as a monk at St David's. Rhigyfarch's Constantine is clearly the *Custennin Gorneu* (=Constantine the Cornishman) of the Welsh genealogies. The genealogy in *Bonedd y Saint*, in its original form, apparently makes Custennyn Gorneu to be the son of Erbin the son of Geraint, and so to be the brother of Selyf (Selevan, patron of St Levan near the Land's End) and uncle of S. Cuby.[11] We note that

[10] At a much later period S. Constantine came to be regarded as one of King Arthur's knights. In Harding's *Metrical Chronicle* he appears as

"Duke Cador's son of Cornwall bounteous
Afore had been one of the table round
In Arthure's time."

[11] See A. W. Wade-Evans, *Life of St. David* (1923), pp. 98, 99.

the Welsh pronunciation of the name resembles the traditional Cornish *Constenton*, with the accent on the second syllable. There is a Llangystennin in Carnarvonshire, close to a parish called Llangernyw, and another in Herefordshire, now called Welsh Bicknor, and he was also honoured at Cosmeston by Llandough-juxta-Cardiff.[12]

The Irish Tradition

In Ireland we find the same tradition of a Constantine who lived there as a monk, after being a king among the Britons. Unfortunately the Irish tradition of S. Constantine is a very confused one, showing signs of an attempt to amalgamate several different traditions, coming from different sources.

The *Félire* of Oengus, on March 10, commemorates a Constantine whom it identifies with the emperor of that name.[13] On March 11 it commemorates "Constantine, King, of Rathin." The *Félire* dates from the beginning of the ninth century. In many manuscripts notes have been added by later writers to try to explain who this Constantine was. They tell us that he was a "king of Britain," and add "he was also king of Scotland." Here we have an obvious attempt to combine two different traditions. These notes to the *Félire* are mostly copied from another Irish book, known as the *Indarba Mochuda a Raithin* (=The Expulsion of Mochuda from Rahan). The *Indarba* says "It was he who marked out the church of Rahen, and dug [the mound for] it, and cultivated 'Constantine's Plot' to the south of Rahen, and Magh Constantin (=Constantine's Plain) on the bank of the Brosny at Ath Maighne."[14]

The Martyrology of Tallaght speaks of "Constantine, a Briton, or the son of Fergus of the Picts." Here we see very clearly the author's hesitation in face of two traditions about Constantine. The Martyrology of Gorman says "Constantine, the Briton, of lasting grace," and the seventeenth-century

[12] Llandough=Lan Docco. S. Docco is identified with S. Cyngar. Now Cyngar appears in the *Life of S. Cuby* as a relative of Cuby, and therefore of Constantine. [Canon Doble discusses the identity of Docco and Cyngar in his *Saint Congar*, and comes to a different conclusion.—*Ed.*]

[13] The feast of "St. Constantine the Emperor" is not found in any other Western liturgical book. It is found in the East, but not on this date.

[14] Plummer's translation.—Rathin is now *Rahan*, in Offaly (Barony of Ballycowan). An Irish writer called Rumann Mac Colmain (d. 747) says that Constantine cleared a large tract of land near Rahen which was called Magh-Constantine (=Constantine's Plain) on which was a church called Cell-Belaige.

commentary adds "Constantine son of Fergus of the Picts, or, according to others, a Briton, abbot of Raithen mo Chuta."

The *Annals of Ulster* has, for the year 588, the entry "Conversion of Constantine to the Lord."

Finally, an Irish writer copied by Colgan in the seventeenth century, tells us that "Constantine, king of the Britons, gave up his kingdom, and came for the sake of pilgrimage to Rahen in the time of S. Mochuda. For he was the successor of S. Mochuda at Rahen, and before that he was king of Alban (Scotland)."[15]

The Scottish Tradition

In Scotland we find a similar tradition, worked up into a regular romance, in the Breviary of Aberdeen, which commemorates "Constantine, King, Monk and Martyr" on March 11. I give the lections in full.

Constantine, son of Paternus, king of Cornubia [Cornwall], married the daughter of the king of Lesser Britain [Brittany]. But behold, by ill fortune the queen died: and the king, greiving over her death and refusing to be comforted, handed over the charge of the kingdom to his son, and then, bidding farewell to all, he left the kingdom and crossed to Ireland; coming to a certain house of religion, he humbly undertook a menial task, which consisted in carrying to the mill each week the grain to be ground, and bringing it back, thus descending from a throne to a mill. But one day Constantine the Miller, sitting in the mill, and not seeing anyone there, said, "Am I Constantine, king of Cornwall, whose head has so often worn the helmet and his body the breastplate?" "No," he replied. As he talked thus with himself, a certain man who was hiding in the mill heard him, and told the abbot what he had heard. When this news spread, all [the monks] run to him and, taking him away from the mill, lead him to the cloister, teach him letters and, by the inspiration of the Holy Ghost, raise him to the priesthood. Soon after he said goodbye to them all, left that place and went to S. Columba, a man most dear to God; and afterwards he was sent by S. Kentigern to Galvedia [Galloway] to preach the word of God, where he was elected abbot, and studied to reform by word and example the flock committed to him. And at last, when Constantine had reached a decrepit old age, he desired of the Lord, what he had long had in his mind, namely that he might die as a martyr for the Church of Christ, and he heard a voice from Heaven saying that it should be as he had asked. And when the man of God had gone over all that country in every direction preaching the word of God, and was staying in the island of Kintyre, certain malignant men came together and hastened to the island that they might wickedly perform that for which the man of God had piously prayed. Coming

[15] Forbes, in his *Kalendars of Scottish Saints*, says that Constantine, son of Fergus King of the Picts, succeeded Mochuda at Rathin after 630. See J. O'Hanlon, *Lives of the Irish Saints*, vol. iii, pp. 318–325.

therefore to the man of God, they cut off the hand of his attendant (*ministri*), which he at once healed by merely touching it. Raging therefore against the man of God, they showered blows upon him, and, among other deadly wounds, they cut off his arm, and leaving him as dead they went away. Then the saint, calling his brethren, comforted them in the spirit of charity, and so fell asleep in the presence of the brethren, and is deservedly counted among the saints and elect martyrs of God. Now he died about the year of our Lord 576[16].

The *Scotichronicon* of John Fordun follows the same tradition as the Breviary of Aberdeen. It tells us that Constantine "was a contemporary of S. Columba," that "he preached the faith to the Scots and Picts. He founded the monastery of brethren at Govane by the Clyde, over whom he ruled as abbot. He converted the whole land of Kintyre, where he died as a martyr, and was buried in his monastery at Govane."[17] Hector Boethius, the Scottish historian, speaks of him and says that there were several churches in Scotland dedicated to him. He found his way even into German martyrologies.[18]

As Jocelyn's Life of S. Kentigern mentions a S. Constantine who was son of a king of the Cambrian Britons of Strathclyde, it is probable that the Constantine honoured in Scotland is a different person from the Cornish Constantine; but later identified with him, as he is honoured on the same day.[19]

§

I think, therefore, we may conclude that some local Cornish chieftain became a monk and founded churches in Devon and Cornwall, one at least of which was of considerable importance

[16] Cf. *Breviarium Aberdonense*, Edinburgh, 1509–10 (facsimile edn., London, 1854. Vol. II, fo. lxvii).

[17] Govan is on the Clyde. I need scarcely say that no biographer of S. Columba mentions Constantine.

[18] In the *Registrum Glasg.* (i. 122) a Kirkconstantine is mentioned, and we find that Kenneil (or *Kennoul*) near Perth and Dunnechtyn (or *Dunnichen*) are dedicated to him. David Laing, in his *Martyrology for the use of the Church of Aberdeen*, mentions S. Cousland's Fair at Dunnechtan. S. Cowstin in Stornoway and S. Constantine at Inverness are dedicated to a later Constantine. The *Kalendar of Drummond*, under March 11, has "in Ireland the holy confessors Libren, Senan, Constantine and Oengus went to Christ." The *Kalendar of Arbuthnott* has "Saint Constantine, King and Martyr" under March 11. His feast in the Breviary of Aberdeen has nine lessons and a collect.

[19] F. G. Holweck (*Biographical Dictionary of the Saints*) mentions King Constantine II, son of Kenneth, who died fighting against the Danes in 874, as commemorated on March 11. Some Western martyrologies, of no very great authority, commemorate a "Constantine, Confessor at Carthage." on the same date. So the name has given rise altogether to one of the most fearful series of muddles in the whole history of hagiography.

and survived as a monastic community down to the end of the eleventh century. He was regarded as one of the chief saints of Dumnonia and became a pan-Celtic saint.[20] The traditions about his conversion from a wild and violent life remind us of the power to overawe and convert the most hardened sinners which Christians in the ages of faith possessed (one thinks of the story of S. Bernard and the duke of Aquitaine) and which we seem to have lost.

[20] S. Constantine appears in the Breton *Life of Turiavus*, bishop of Dol; and in the Life of S. Ninnoc, in the Cartulary of Quimperlé, we find a princess "of the race of the Scots, a daughter of King Constantine, of the kindred of Julian Caesar, named Meneduc," as the wife of King Brochanus!

SAINT DECUMAN*

VENERATED AT DEGIBMA, NEAR HELSTON

ONE of the most interesting clues to the early history of the west of England may be found in the long line of Celtic dedications which stretches across the north of Somerset. Beginning with Culbone, where the patron saint is the famous Irish missionary S. Columban, in the west, we come at once to Porlock, where the church is dedicated to the Welsh saint Dubricius. South-east of Porlock is Timberscombe, dedicated to S. Petroc, the chief saint of Devon and Cornwall. A little further east is Carhampton, the site of a once famous monastery founded by S. Carantoc, a Cardigan monk who also built churches at Crantock in Cornwall, and at Carantec and Tregarantec in Brittany. Next to Carhampton is Watchet, where S. Decuman is honoured. Not far away is Wick, where there is a holy well of S. Sidwell, the patron of a parish in the Celtic half of Exeter, while at Over Stowey is S. David's holy well. Further east we find the Cornish S. Kew at Kewstoke, and S. Congar at Congresbury and Badgworth. Near Glastonbury S. Gildas is the patron of the parish of Street, which once contained a place called *Lan-to-kai* (=Monastery of Kea). S. Patern is said to have been the original patron of Nailsea, and S. Bridget of Chelvey.[1] The progress of historical research will probably add to this list of Celtic dedications. They present a series of problems the solution of which would help us to know what was happening in Somerset in the two hundred years which preceded its conquest by the West Saxons.[2]

* Cornish Saints Series, no. 28 (1932). First published in *A History of Watchet Church*, by F. C. Eeles (1932).

[1] On Brandon Hill in Bristol once stood a chapel of the great Irish saint Brendan. The church of Brendon in Devon, close to Oare and Culbone, is also dedicated to him. There is a parish called *Withiel* Florey, not far from Watchet, which suggests the Withiel in Cornwall. It is "possibly a personal name" (C. Henderson in *Cornish Church Guide*). Bristol itself may mean *St Bride's Stow*. There was an altar of S. David in Wells Cathedral (Bishop Cornish in 1513 desired to be buried between the altars of Holy Cross and S. David); and a "store of S. David" at Winsford in 1532 (" in stauro S. David viiid" is in a will dated March 12 that year). There was an altar of S. Nectan in Cheddar church in 1493, as Thomas More desired to be buried before his altar. There was also at Cheddar a chapel of another Celtic saint, S. Columban, distinct from the parish church. (I am indebted to Mr M. H. N. Cuthbert Atchley for these interesting facts).

[2] The following Celtic saints are found in Somerset kalendars, and therefore preserved their cult throughout the middle ages: Carantoc, Petroc, Decuman, Brigid, Samson, Columban, Congar, David, Nonita, Nectan, Judoc and Machutus. S. Nonita was honoured at Wells on March 3; this saint has been identified (perhaps wrongly) with Nonna, the supposed mother of S. David. The influence of continental kalendars probably introduced the cult of S. Judoc and S. Machutus (Malo).

Two of these Celtic saints, S. Decuman and S. Congar, have ancient Latin Lives written in Somerset. I give a translation of the Life of S. Decuman, printed in the *Nova Legenda Anglie* by Wynkyn de Worde in 1516.[3] [A seventeenth-century manuscript in the library at Wells (the date seems to be about 1680), printed by Prebendary Reynolds in *Wells Cathedral: its foundation, constitutional history and statutes* (p. clxviii), contains an abbreviated version of this *Vita* in the original Latin, word for word the same as that printed in *Nova Legenda Anglie* except that large excisions have been made. The transcriber introduces it with the words: "Before I leave this Chapter I shall give the Reader what I have mett with in an old Legend of St Decuman, which gives the name to a little village, neere Watchet, on the North Sea, in the West of this Countie of Somersett and consequently to a praebend of this Church:—

De Sancto Decumano Heremita et Martyre. Beatus Decumanus," &c.]

Of Saint Decuman Hermit and Martyr

The blessed Decuman sprang from illustrious stock in the western parts of Cambria, which is now called Wales (*Wallia*), from parents who were conspicuous for their devotion to the Christian religion. For that nation [i.e., the Welsh] laid aside its barbarian savagery and forsook the error of the Gentiles, was initiated by life-giving sacraments and speedily submitted to Christ, and was illuminated by the doctrines of the Gospel, before Greater Britain, which now is England [became Christian]. And therein many did shine forth glorious in faith, eminent in virtue, glittering with miracles. Among whom did Decuman, chastely brought up, instructed in the Catholic faith, appear like the day star among lesser stars, possessing a reputation for perfect integrity. After he had passed childhood's years at home, still preserving his innocence he grew to be a young man of excellent disposition, and never let his imagination wander abroad [into what is unlawful], as many do, but most carefully restrained himself by keeping the rules of discipline. Indeed precepts quickly have their due effect where grace affords its help and obedience lightens [the observance of] commands. For he was pure in speech, letting no wanton word, and no idle word, if he could help it, pass his lips, but only that which was calculated to edify others. In eating and drinking he kept the due mean of true temperance, lest by excess of abstinence he might be accused of superstition, or by eating too much might suffer gluttony to weigh down [his soul]. And while the other young men of the same age as the blessed Decuman were devoted to the various delights of the chase, or occupied with other pursuits and occupations, he, spurning every carnal delight, compelled his flesh to serve the spirit, and studiously frequented churches, and what he heard [there] from the divine

[3] ed. Horstman (Oxford, 1901), vol. i, pp. 263–5.

scriptures he did with great ardour commit to memory. Without encumbering himself with too much learning, he had given himself up entirely to the pursuit of holiness, and, so far as he was able without incurring the ridicule of the courtiers, he had devoted himself to contemplation. For works teach better than words of learning, holiness understands [the truth] better than disputation, and he who loves most knows most. In truth Saint Decuman, prevented by the ardour of the Holy Ghost, was already revolving in his mind the high designs to which afterwards he gave effect. And, indeed, he would have fulfilled his pious desires even then, but he was waiting for the tumult of the multitude and the wantonness of his fellow-tribesmen, whom he thoroughly detested, to cease. For "no prophet is accepted in his own country" [Luke 4: 24], and "a man's foes shall be they of his own household" [Matt. 10: 36]. So, for fear of being a stumbling-block [to the thoughtless], he refrained, and committing himself wholly to God alone, postponed for a time the fulfilment of his pious purpose.

At length, observing the time, and finding an opportunity for a secret flight, he made his way to the Severn Sea, without the knowledge of any of his friends, taking special care to keep in ignorance his constant companions and those who seemed most closely bound to him by ties of a common zeal for study, taking Christ only as his confidant and guide. Why need I say more? He had neither ship to sail in nor money to pay his passage, and it was necessary to provide against his being pursued. The man of God, trusting in the mercy of God and not doubting of his power [to help him], gathered together into a faggot the twigs he found growing in a thicket by the sea, and using them as a support, launched out into the deep. And so, by the governance of the divine providence, he arrived at the opposite shore near Dunster Castle (*castrum Durostorum*). These are thy works, O Christ, who dost thus deal wondrously with thy saints. Truly "Thy ways are in the sea and thy paths in many waters" [Ps. 77: 19]. At the time when Saint Decuman, divinely guided, came into England, there was in that part of the country in which he landed a vast solitude, suitable for the abode of a hermit (*vasta heremi solitudo*) covered with thickets and thorn bushes, with dense woods stretching far and wide, lofty mountains, and hollow valleys between them. This site pleased him, it seemed fitted for his pious purpose, so that in very truth he seemed to say, "This shall be my rest for ever, here will I dwell, for I have chosen it" [Ps. 132: 15]. So then the holy man, having exchanged his native land for exile, and the luxury of a palace for the caves of the desert, began to abide there, living on herbs and roots, and devoting himself to frequent fasts and prayers, taming his flesh with a hair shirt and afflicting his body with vigils: and in proportion as he consorted rarely with men was he frequently comforted and inspired by the conversation of angels.[4] Thus leading the life of a hermit he had lived many years in the aforesaid solitude. He is reported also to have had a cow whose milk supplied him with frugal sustenance, as bodily necessity required, at least on the chief festivals, as it is read of the blessed Giles that he had a hind which provided him with milk. Nor did the saint lack fierce and unexpected persecution. For "all they that will live godly in Christ shall suffer persecution" [2 Tim. 3: 12]: for this life did Christ leave to his fellow-heirs, as it is read in the Gospel, "If

[4] Cf. the *Imitation of Christ*, bk i, c. 20, 6.

they have persecuted me, they will also persecute you" [John 15: 20]. And the Apostle, too, says, "we must through many tribulations enter into the kingdom of God" [Acts 14: 22]. For as the furnace to gold, and the file to iron, and the flail to grain, so is tribulation to the righteous man. When therefore Saint Decuman had worked many signs and miracles, which by the negligence of chroniclers have been almost entirely forgotten in our country—otherwise by the gift of God they would have been preserved for our edification—a certain man, a man of Belial, more venomous than the asp, more poisonous than the adder, envying this great father's sanctity, hating virtue and raging with furious mind in detestation of the Christian name, approached like a wild beast and cut off the head of the saint of the Lord amid his prayers and holy devotions, and so sent him to the heavenly kingdom. By such martyrdom therefore did he go hence to the Lord, after so many and so great penances which he had inflicted on his body, that he might the more evidently show by his example that [the way to Heaven] is not a passage from [earthly] delights to [heavenly] delights, but they who wish to live according to the Gospel—the whole of their life must be a cross and a martyrdom[5]. For he is too delicate a soldier who wishes to rejoice here with the world and hereafter to reign with Christ[6].

But this also is not to be passed over in silence—that when he was beheaded with a certain *vanga*, the trunk of the mutilated body, they say, raised itself and took its own head in its hands and carried it from the place where he was beheaded to a fountain of most limpid water, in which he was accustomed to wash his face with his hands. Which to this day in memory and reverence of him is called the "Fountain of Saint Decuman," and is sweet, healthful, and necessary to the inhabitants for drinking purposes.[7] In which place the head, together with the body, were afterwards sought for and found by the faithful, and honourably placed in a tomb. [Thus] ancient miracles are renewed, and the signs which the Lord deigned to work by the merits of the most blessed Dionysius of the Gauls once more take place[8] to the praise and glory of his most holy name, who liveth and reigneth through immortal ages of ages. Amen.

In dealing with ancient Latin Lives of saints, it is necessary first to try to answer the question, Where and when was the Life written?

[5] *tota vita sua fiat crux et martyrium.* A quotation from the *Imitation of Christ*, bk. ii, c. 12, 7: "Tota vita Christi crux fuit et martyrium."

[6] *Hic gaudere cum mundo et in futurum regnare cum Christo.* A quotation from the same, i, 24, 6: "Ecce vere non potes duo gaudia habere, delectari hic in mundo, et postea regnare cum Christo."

[7] S. Decuman's well is on the hill side, within a stone's throw of the parish church of S. Decuman at Watchet. Dom Ethelbert Horne says that there is a holy well of S. Decuman at Williton, a mile or two south of Watchet. It "is in a field at the west end of the church, and the water comes out between great stones set on end, having a third forming a roof on the top of them. As the water runs down the sharply sloping field it flows into a number of stone basins, one below the other. The water is still sought after by the inhabitants, or was when I saw this curious spring in September 1914." (*Holy Wells of Somerset*, p. 50). But Dom Horne made a slip here: the holy well is at S. Decuman's, *not* at Williton.

[8] S. Denys (Dionysius), first bishop of Paris, is said to have carried his head after his execution to the site of the present abbey of Saint-Denys.

It is perfectly clear that this Life of S. Decuman is a Somerset composition. The writer mentions Dunster Castle, and he is familiar with the local traditions of Watchet and Williton. He might be a monk of Dunster, where there was a small monastery, a cell of the great Benedictine abbey of Bath. As, however, the name of S. Decuman is not found in the kalendar of Dunster there cannot have been any cult of him in the priory there, and it is more likely that the author of his Life was either a monk of Muchelney Abbey, or a canon of Wells Cathedral[9]—probably the latter, as the church of S. Decuman at Watchet was given as a prebend to Wells by Simon Brito at the end of the twelfth century. Our author is a devout student, very fond of the legends of the saints, and of the *Imitation of Christ*, from which he culls two direct quotations (another passage contains a clear reference to the *Imitation*, though it is not a verbal citation). Other pious reflexions with which he fills up the gaps in the very meagre stock of traditions at his disposal might be traced to similar sources; he may have copied them from a medieval "commonplace-book." The fact that he quotes from the *Imitation*, of which the earliest known copy dates from 1425, shows that he lived in the fifteenth century, or perhaps even in the beginning of the sixteenth century. His *Life of S. Decuman* is, in fact, one of the latest additions to the *Nova Legenda Anglie*.[10]

It is possible that our author knew of the existence of a parish in Pembrokeshire dedicated to S. Degeman, as he says that his hero came from "the *western* parts of Cambria," but all the rest of his description of the saint's life in his native country he drew from his own imagination. He has very little more to help him when he has brought Decuman to Somerset. It is clear that the real story of his life had long been forgotten at Watchet—our

[9] The name of S. Decuman is found on August 30 in the Colour-list of Wells and Calendar of Muchelney, and a collect for his feast is found on a leaf torn from a 15th-century Wells breviary. See *Muchelney Memoranda*, by the Dean of Wells, pp. 7, 16, 42. It is to be noted that the feast of S. Decuman was a *principal feast* at Muchelney, as were the feasts of S. Giles and S. Denys, both referred to in this Life.

[10] It belongs to a series of fifteen new Lives added to the *Nova Legenda Anglie* by Wynkyn de Worde for his new edition of that work in 1516. Horstman says "of these new lives, those of Cungar and Decuman are late works of the fourteenth century, as is proved by the alliteration." (As a matter of fact, the *Life of S. Decuman* is later than the fourteenth century, as I have shown, while the Dean of Wells has discovered a twelfth-century fragment of the *Life of S. Congar*.) Baring-Gould and Fisher are therefore in error in saying (*Lives of the British Saints*, vol. ii, p. 323) that the *Vita* is by John of Tynemouth, and that it "is an epitome of a Life now lost."

author himself complains of the scarcity of information concerning him. All he can find is the story of the faggot, the tradition about the holy well, and the story of the saint's cow. Each of these is a piece of "common form," found in the Lives of numerous Cornish saints. S. Ia, for example, crosses the sea from Ireland on a leaf, S. Piran on a mill-stone, and S. Ilic on a hurdle; cows appear in the Lives of S. Cuby and S. Endelienta; and the story of S. Decuman carrying his head to the holy well after his martyrdom is a repetition of an exactly similar incident in the legend of S. Nectan.

I fear, then, we must conclude that, beyond the witness which it gives to the vitality of the cult of this Welsh saint at Watchet, the Life I have translated does not tell us anything about S. Decuman.[11] But we have another and surer source of information. M. Loth has said that "in these three countries (Wales, Cornwall and Brittany) it is not the Lives of the saints that tell us most about the existence of the saints and the national organization of religion, but the *names of places*."

The study of place-names shows us that S. Decuman, instead of being, as his Life asserts, a hermit, whose whole existence was passed in a wilderness, was in reality an active missionary and organizer of Celtic monasteries, whose activities spread over central and south Wales, north Somerset, and west Cornwall.

In Wales we find his name at the chapel of Llanddegyman, in the parish of Llanfihangel Cwmdu, in Breconshire.[12] Now we

[11] Camden had obviously seen this Life, and quotes from it in his description of Somerset. He says: "Near the castle of Dunster aforesaid, are two small villages, dedicated to two of their Country saints: Carenton is the name of the one, from Carentocus the Britain; the other, St Decombes, from Decumanus, who setting sail out of South Wales, landed here (as we find in an ancient Agonal) in a horrid desert full of shrubs and briars, the woods thick and close, stretched out a vast way both in length and breadth, strutting up with lofty mountains, severed wonderfully by the hollow vallies. Here, having bid farewell to the vanities of the world, he was stab'd by an Assassin, and so got the reputation of a Saint among the common people" (*Magna Britannia*, vol. i, col. 69, ed. 1753). In Wilson's Martyrology we find under August 27 "In Anglia S. Decumani eremitae et martyris." He is commemorated on August 30 in a Norwich martyrology of the fifteenth century (Cotton MS. Julius B.VII: the words "et sancti decimani martiris "are added at the end of the entry for August 30;) and in the Welsh kalendar (apparently written for Llandaff) in Cott. Vesp. A.XIV., August 30 is the feast "Sancti Decumanni conf[essoris]." Nicholas Roscarrock, a West-Country writer of Queen Elizabeth's reign, also gives August 30 as his day. Baring-Gould and Fisher say that the Altemps Martyrology (13-cent.) commemorates him on August 27 but they are clearly wrong in saying that his name is in "the Bath Kalendar." The kalendar to which they refer is really that of the priory of Dunster, which was a cell of Bath Abbey, and, as we have seen, it does *not* contain his name. S. Decuman is also mentioned by Wion and Castellanus, and in Alford's *Annales*. No other writer mentions our saint. (See the Bollandist *Acta Sanctorum*, under August 27.)

[12] A. W. Wade-Evans, *Parochiale Wallicanum*, p. 19.

know that from Brecknock went forth numerous missionaries who evangelized Herefordshire to the east and Glamorgan, Carmarthen and Pembroke to the south and west. Consequently we are not surprised to find that S. Degeman is the patron of the parish of Rhoscrowther or Rhos Gylyddwr, otherwise Llanddegyman, in southern Pembrokeshire.[13] He is also said to have been the original patron of the adjoining parish of Pwll-crochan.[14]

Now Rhoscrowther was once a very important monastery. In the Laws of Howel the Good we find that "there are seven bishop-houses (*esgobdy*) in Dyved; and Mynyw (=St David's) is the chief in Wales, Llan Ismael (=St Ishmael's), and Llan Degeman, and Llan Ussylt (St Issel's), and Llan Teilaw (Llandeilo near Maenclochog), and Llan Teulydawc (Llandeulyddog in Carmarthen) and Llan Geneu. The abbots of Teilaw and Teulydawc and Ismael and Degeman should be ordained scholars. Twelve pounds is the heriot of every one of these, and to the Lord of Dyved it is paid . . . . Whosoever shall affront one of those abbots, let him pay seven pounds to him, and let there be a washer-woman from his kindred, as a reproach to the kindred and as a memorial of the vengeance." Mr Wade-Evans observes "What precisely is meant by *bishop-house* does not appear, but the monastic character of the system is clear."[14a] Abbey-bishoprics are found everywhere in Wales, Ireland, Cornwall and Brittany before the introduction of the system of diocesan bishoprics in those lands.

The churches of Rhoscrowther and Pwllcrochan are both highly interesting, though they do not seem to contain any work earlier than the middle ages. "A short distance to the south-west of the church of Rhoscrowther," Mr G. E. Evans tells me, "is St Decuman's well. Any protection or covering to the well has disappeared. On the tithe schedule it is called St Agnes' Well."[15] In *South Wales* (Little Guide series, by G. W. and J. H. Wade) I read that "at the W. of the church, on the S. side, there is a curious little cell with a piscina and a small opening communicating with the exterior of the building." Can this have been an

[13] *ib.* p. 12. We find, Professor Mawer tells me, the forms Llan Degman, Llan Degeman and Eglwys Degemann.
[14] *Arch. Camb.*, 1888, p. 127.
[14a] *Life of S. David*, pp.11-9 pp. 94-95.
[15] The well was believed to possess healing powers. See Fenton's *Pembrokeshire* (1811), p. 400.

anchoret's cell preserving the tradition of a former monastery?

From Rhoscrowther, which must have been his chief foundation, Decuman evangelized, not only north Somerset,[16] but also the extreme west of Cornwall. A chapel bearing his name existed in the middle ages at Degibma (the word=Degaman), in the parish of Wendron, near the Lizard. In 1397 Simon Body, vicar of Wendron, obtained a licence from Bishop Stafford of Exeter to say Mass in the chapel of S. Decuman in his parish once a year, *viz.*, on the feast day of the saint. Degibma is on the Loe pool, which must at this period, before the formation of the Loe bar, have been a tidal estuary—just the place where we should expect to find the chapel of a Celtic saint. C. G. Henderson, who was the first to identify the chapel of S. Decuman with Degibma, has also discovered that there was another Degibma near Burthogg, in Crowan. He thinks, too, that Decon Downs (*Decam* 1753, *Decum* 1756) might perhaps take its name from our saint, and it is remarkable that at Watchet the name should be written *Decom* in 1418.

It is worthy of notice that touching Rhoscrowther parish in Pembrokeshire we find the parish of St Petrox or Llanbedrog. Now S. Petroc is the chief of the Cornish saints, the patron of Padstow and Bodmin and at least 25 other churches and chapels in Devon and Cornwall, and of Timberscombe (near Watchet, be it observed) in Somerset. It looks as if Decuman and Petroc were associated together. Stanton in his *Menology* (p. 414), probably following the advice of Edmund Bishop, says that "Decuman is also called Decombe and Dagan." Now Leland, quoting from the *De sepultura sanctorum anglorum*, tells us that "Credan, Medan and *Dachan* [or *Dachuna*], men illustrious by sanctity of life, and imitators of Petrock, were buried at Bosmanach" (Bodmin).[17] It is interesting to note that a S. Credan, by tradition an early abbot of Evesham, was honoured at Wells (*Muchelney Memoranda*, p. 12).

Thus it looks as if S. Decuman belonged to a group of Brecon saints who founded monasteries in south-west Wales, from

[16] A charter of King John on behalf of the Cistercian abbey of Neath speaks of land "inter ecclesiam sancti Decumani et Kanesford" (*Monasticon*, vol. v, p. 260). (Kanesford is a house a short distance south-west of S. Decuman's church). The Calendar of Inquisitiones post mortem in 1274 mentions the church of S. Decuman at Watchet, the Feet of Fines for 1418 calls it *Seynt Decom*. In 1549 it is *Saincte Decomans*.

[17] Williton church is now dedicated to S. Peter, but the original patron might possibly have been S. Petroc.

which missions to Somerset and Cornwall were sent out. As Watchet is so near Carhampton, and not far from Timberscombe, while Rhoscrowther immediately adjoins St Petrox, he may have been associated with the great saints of Cardigan and Pembroke, Carantoc, Petroc and Brioc, who did such an important work in Somerset, Cornwall and Brittany.

The word *decumanus* (a commoner form than *decimanus*) meant in Latin "a farmer of tithes." *Miles decumanus* meant "a soldier of the tenth cohort." It is clear that Saint Decuman must have been a romanized Briton.

§

[There appear to be no remains of S. Decuman's chapel on the Loe pool at Helston today, and no evidence has been found of any chapel at the Degibma in Crowan parish. It is stated in more than one History of Cornwall that S. Euny's chapel at Mertheruny in Wendron was also under Decuman's patronage, but Charles Henderson has shown that this is an error. He adds that:] "On the south side of the town of Padstow, where the main road ascends, is a house called 'St Decuman's,' which appears to be identical with the tenement of 'St Edmonds,' named in the parish map of 1840. It is supposed that *Edmond's* is a corruption of *Decuman's*. It is possible that there was a chapel of St Decuman here, but there is no historical evidence of it, or, for that matter, of a St Edmond's chapel. Padstow, however, was full of chapels and oratories before the Reformation. A deed of 1535 refers to a garden in *Berylond juxta lapidem Withymon* in the town of Padstow. Can this be a corruption of *Decuman*?"

Collect for S. Decuman's Feast

O God, who art the defence, the strength and the crown of the innocent, grant unto us that we may be both instructed by the examples of blessed Decuman thy martyr and aided by his prayers. Through our Lord.

Deus qui es propugnaculum, fortitudo et corona innocencium, da nobis beati Decumani martiris tui et exemplis instrui et precibus adiuuari. Per dominum.[18]

[18] From the Wells Breviary of the fifteenth century, quoted by J. Armitage Robinson in the *Journal of Theological Studies*, vol. xxix (1928), p. 137.

SAINT MAWGAN*

Patron of the Mawgans

THERE are two parishes in Cornwall called Mawgan, namely, Mawgan-in-Pydar and Mawgan-in-Meneage. *Mawgan* is a personal name, the original form of which was *Malcan* or *Malcant*, which, Joseph Loth pointed out[1] is "a typical British name," and the two Cornish parishes of Mawgan are called after a saint of that name, who is honoured in Wales and in Brittany. Mawgan-in-Pydar is called *Saint Mauchan of Lanhern* in 1257,[2] and Mawgan-in-Meneage appears in Domesday as *Saint Mawan.*

Unfortunately no Life of S. Mawgan has come down to us. Nicholas Roscarrock, the devoted Cornish hagiologist of the sixteenth century, made the following note in the manuscript book which he wrote on the subject: "Sainct Maugan, saith Rowse in a Catalogue of Brittaine Sts. wch. I have seen, was Bishop of the Iles of Scilly." But, with the exception of this very late and doubtful statement, all local traditions about him have perished, not only in Cornwall, but also in the other Celtic countries I have mentioned, and we are obliged to depend entirely on the information to be obtained from three other sources at our disposal, *viz*., the mention of the saint's name in liturgical books, references to him in the Lives of other saints and in Welsh literature, and the evidence of place-names in Wales, Cornwall and Brittany.

It will help us best to understand the problem if we deal with the topographical evidence first.

In Wales Saint *Meugan* is honoured at Capel Meugan in the parish of Llandegfan in Anglesey, on the Menai Straits;[3] at

* Cornish Saints Series, no. 39 (revised edition, 1936; the first edition bears the same date).

[1] "nom parfaitment brittonique," *Noms des saints bretons*, p. 89.

[2] Ecclesia de La Herne 1279, Ecclesia Sancti Maugani 1288, Ecclesia beatorum Nicholai et Maugani de Lanherne 1309.

[3] The chapel "stood in a field near Plas Meugan". (The latter is a modern name, but there are ancient names [Gorsedd Meugan and Dinas Meugan] commemorating him in the parish.) According to Richard Llwyd (*Poetical Works*, London, 1837, pp. 24–25, note) S. Meugan's festival was observed here on September 25. Browne Willis (*Bangor*, 1721, pp. 278, 281) says so too: "The chapel gradually fell into decay after the founding of the chantry of our Lady of Beaumaris." (Baring-Gould and Fisher, *Lives of the British Saints*, vol. iii, pp. 479–480).

Llanfeugan,[4] also called Llanrhudd (=the Red Church), the mother church of Ruthin in Denbighshire; at Llanfeugan[5] near Hay in Brecknock; at Capel Meugan near Cilymaenllwyd in Carmarthenshire; and at Llanfeugan in Kemes, in north-east Pembrokeshire. The latter was clearly the principal centre of his cult. It must have been a famous place of pilgrimage in the middle ages, and was still visited by pilgrims at the end of the sixteenth century, as we see by a letter from the Privy Council ordering its demolition in 1592.

> Wheras we have received l'res [letters] from the lordes and others of her mates [majesty's] most honorable privie counsell to us and others directed, wherbie we ar willed & requiered to Informe or selves of all places wth in this Countie of Pembrooke where in tymes past there have beene pilgrimages, Images, or offringes, wher unto (As their lps [lordships] ar Informed) divers sortes of people do use to repaire as well in the night season, as other tymes of the daie & that in great nombers, and that we sholde cause thos Idolatrous & superstitious monumentes to be pulled downe, broken & quite defaced, so as there be no monument, token or memorie remayning of the same & likewise to take order that herafter there be no such unlawfull resorte to thos supersticious places, but to appoint some discrete & well affected persons to have an eie & regarde to thos that notw[ith]standing this Inhibicion shall repaire to thos places, and to se them apprehended & brought before us, to be severelie punished for their disobedience & lewde behavior. Thes are therefore by vertue & authoritie of the said honorable l'res & commission to will and requier you being gent'men to us knowne to be well affected & forwarde in her mates service & good of the countrie, forthwth w all convenient spede to repaire to the place called St meygans wher somtyme offringes & supersticious pilgrymages have bene used, and there to cause to be pulled downe & utterlie defaced all relques & monumentes of that chappell, not leaving one stone thereof upon an other, & from tyme to tyme to cause to be apprehended all such persone & persones of what sexe kinde or sorte whatsoeuer; that shall presume herafter contarie to the tenor and prporte of the said honorable commission, to repaire either by night or daie to the said chappell or well in supersticious maner & them to bring or sende before us or anie of us, to be used & dealt wth all according to their desertes. hereof praying you to have speciall regarde for the due accomplisment of the premisses, as you tender the service of god & her

[4] *Pant Meugan Ucha* and *Isa* "occur in the *Ruthin Castle Papers*, as the names, in the sixteenth and eighteenth centuries, of a tract of land lying in the adjoining parish of Llanfwrog. . . . Tir Meugan, at Bathafarn, is mentioned as boundary land in an account of the perambulation, in 1810, of the adjoining parish of Llanfair. . . . Bodeugan, one of the townships of St Asaph parish, probably stands for Bod Feugan" (L.B.S., iii, 479). Browne Willis gives the festival at Llanrhudd as September 25.

[5] Also *Llanfigan*. In the *Taxatio* of 1219 it is called *Eccl'ia de Sco. Mengano*. Browne Willis says the festival is September 23. The patron saint is now S. Nicholas (cf. note 2).

matie & the benefit and quiet of the countrie. we take o[u]r leave commending you to godes tuicion.

hauerford west, this xiiijth of July . . . 1592
Yor very loving ffrendes
George Owen
Albane Stepneth
John' ap Res.

[to Robert] Vaghan gen'
John' Garmons gent.
Owen ph'es of penbedo gen'
Thomas ap Richarde clerke parsone of penbedo
Jeuan dauid clerke parson of Bridell.
George Owen clerke parson of whitechurche.

The above letter, which is copied from a manuscript in the handwriting of the author, George Owen, preserved in the Vairdre Book *at Bronwydd* (*f.85a.*), *is endorsed*):

To or very loving ffrendes Robert Vaghan, John Garmons & Owen phillppes of penbedo gent; Thomas ap Richard clerke parsone of penbedo, Jeuan Dauid clerke parsone of Bridell & George Owen clerke parsone of whitechurche & to eche and euerie of them.

This document is of the greatest interest for the evidence it affords of the attachment of the native Welsh to ancient Catholic traditions and customs so late as the end of Elizabeth's reign. (One may remark in passing that the use made of the local clergy by the Privy Council in this unjustifiable interference with harmless religious customs which were obviously very dear to the country people must have had much to do with the alienation of the people of Wales from the Established Church. There is no need to point out how greatly this senseless vandalism has hindered the work of the historian and antiquary in later times). The "chapel and well" of S. Meygans appear to have been in the parish of Llanfair Nant Gwyn. It is not quite certain, Professor William Rees tells me, whether it is or is not the same as the "Cappell Meygan in Bridell" mentioned in a list of Pembrokeshire chapels, "formerly erected on account of pilgrimages but now mostly in ruins,"[6] contained in the Kemes Tracts.[7] Several places in the neighbourhood bear the name of Meugan: near Pant y Deri we find *Llanfoygan*, with a spring, a valley and a glen known respectively as Pistyll Meugan, Cwm Meugan and Dyffryn Meugan, while there is a *Trefigan* in Llanrhian. There is a fair called Meugan Fair held at Eglwys Wrw in Kemes, an

[6] *Capellas olim peregrinationis causa erectas, quarum nunc pars maxima dilabuntur.*
[7] Owen's *Pembrokeshire*, part II, . 509.

adjoining parish, on the Monday following November 22 (eleven days after the feast of S. Martin), which is described in a document quoted in Owen's *Pembrokeshire* as "the Mondaye after St Martin's daye, a great faire." (It is curious, we may note in passing, that in Cornwall St Martin-in-Meneage is a parish united with Mawgan). There was also a *Ffair Feigan* at St Dogmael's, a short distance to the north, also in the deanery of Kemes. There is a *Cilfigan* west of Usk in Monmouthshire.

In Cornwall, as we have seen, S. Mawgan is the eponym of two parishes, and the name Mawgan enters into several place-names in other parishes. There is a *Bosmawgan* in St Winnow, in 1389 written *Bodmalgan*. Close by is a *Polmawgan*, and in Lanreath is Castlemawgan (*Castel Mawgan* in 1395). A hill at Trenance in Mullion (not far, we may observe, from Mawgan-in-Meneage) is called *Crick-Mawgan;* and Crigmajor in St Wenn was written *Crukmagon* in 1358 and *Crucmayon* in 1350. In St Ives is *Trevalgan*, and a *Trevelgan* in Mawgan-in-Meneage. The reader will have noticed that two of these place-names bear out Loth's suggestion that Maugan is from *Malgan*. We shall find further evidence of this in Brittany.

In Brittany, S. Maugan is the patron and eponym of a parish in the old diocese of Saint-Malo, between Saint-Méen and Montfort-sur-Meu. It belonged to the abbey of Saint-Jacques de Montfort, and is called the *parochia de Sancto Magaldo* (a slip for Malgando?) in a document of the twelfth century and Saint-Maugand in one of the sixteenth century.[8] I visited the church in July 1935. It is ancient, but not of any special interest. North of the high altar is a statue (? eighteenth-century) of S. Maugan as a bishop, blessing, and wearing surplice, cope and mitre, stole, gloves and pectoral cross. The rector told me that the Sunday after September 24 is their patronal festival, kept as a double of the 1st class.

Three miles or so west of Saint-Brieuc is a parish called *La Méaugon*. Gaultier de Mottay, in his *Iconographie bretonne*, says that the patron saint is "Sanctus Malganus, a disciple of S. Brieuc, according to his legend, sixth century, [feast] nineteenth June. He is represented as a simple monk in a sixteenth-century window at La Méaugon, of which he is patron. We think that this saint is the same as S. Maugan." The *légende* of S. Brioc speaks of a *Marcan*, who is associated with him both in Brittany

[8] See Guillotin de Corson, *Pouillé de Rennes*, vol. ii, p. 664; vi, 168-171.

and in Cornwall,[9] and who is a different person from Mawgan. The latter however seems also to be connected with Brioc. St Meugan in Kemes is only a few miles from Landyfriog, Mawgan-in-Pydar is near St Breoke, while Saint-Maugan lies between Saint-Brieuc-des-Iffs and Saint-Brieuc-de-Mauron, and not far from Merdrignac, where is also a chapel of S. Brioc. La Méaugon, as we have seen, is near the city of Saint-Brieuc, but further evidence, in the shape of early forms of the name and records of its dedication, are necessary before we can feel sure that our saint is the eponym. Loth thought that the name might be a corruption of Lan-Maeocon, and the patron be S. Maeoc (*op. cit.*, p. 86). In the parish of Sainte-Sève, near Morlaix, is a place called Lomogan which, Loth tells us, "certainly contains the name Maugan" (*op. cit.*, p. 89).

Not far from Saint-Maugan, in a southerly direction in the parish of Pleucadeuc, was a seigneurie called Saint-Maugan, and the "Heath of S. Maugan" occupies a large area of the northern part of the parish. It is interesting to find our saint's name in a parish dedicated to S. Cadoc, when we remember that S. Cadoc's chapel and famous holy well in the parish of Padstow, the only place in Cornwall where S. Cadoc is honoured, are quite close to Mawgan-in-Pydar. There is a further connection between these two saints, as we shall see.[10]

S. Maugan has a place, though not a very prominent place, in the liturgical books of Brittany. In the kalendar of a beautifully illuminated Book of Hours dating from the fourteenth or fifteenth century, written for some diocese in the north-east of Brittany,[11] now in the Bibliothèque de l'Arsenal (MS. 616), we find under September 24 the entry "Malgand, bishop" (*Malgandi episcopi*). One other Breton kalendar contains the name of S. Maugan, that of the abbey of Saint-Méen,[12] which was close to

[9] See my *Saint Brioc*. This figure of "S. Meaugan as a monk bearing a pyx" is "unfortunately the sole remaining fragment of the window on the epistle side of the choir, which contained a series of scenes from the life of the saintly eponym of the parish, of whom practically nothing is known" (R. Couffon, "Verrières anciennes des Côtes-du-Nord", in *Mém. de la Soc. d'Em. des C.-du-N.*, 1936, p. 214.

[10] In Scotland "S. Machan, who is commemorated at *Ecclesmachan*, in Linlithgowshire, is said to have been a disciple of S. Cadoc", while "Cambuslang is dedicated to S. Cadoc of Llancarvan" (Watson, *Celtic Place-Names of Scotland*, 1926, pp. 195, 151).

[11] Duine thought it was written for the diocese of Rennes, as the kalendar is rich in saints specially honoured at Rennes. On the other hand S. William of Saint-Brieuc and S. Malo of Alet appear in the litany before S. Melaine and the other Rennes saints. *S. Mevennus* (Méen) is written in the kalendar in blue letters.

[12] In the *Obituaire de S. Méen*, Bibl. Nat., MS. Lat. 9889, September 24 (A manuscript of the 16th cent.).

the parish of Saint-Maugan. He is mentioned simply as a "confessor" (*Malgandi confessoris*). There do not seem to have been proper lessons for his festival; if there were any, they are lost.

Welsh liturgical books are exceedingly rare, their destruction at the Reformation being very thorough, but a certain number of kalendars remain, and they suggest that S. Mawgan must have had a liturgical cult in Wales, for many of them contain his name, and it is significant that the majority commemorate him on September 25 or 26.[13] This fact would seem to indicate that the S. Meugan who is honoured in so many places in Wales is the same as the patron of Saint-Maugan in Brittany, whose day is September 24.

There is still one more proof, and an extremely important one, of the existence of a liturgical cult of S. Mawgan in the early middle ages. The British Museum contains a manuscript (Harl. MS. 863) of Exeter origin, in which is a litany in a handwriting of the eleventh century.[14] In this litany, 319 saints are invoked, and it is surprising to find that barely a dozen of them can be considered Celtic. Even of these, S. Winnoc and S. Judoc do not appear as Breton saints but as saints honoured respectively in Flanders and at Winchester (the former, who died abbot of Wormhout, is in a group of Netherland saints, and the latter, some of whose relics were at Winchester, follows S. Swithun), and I think that S. Neot owes his place in the litany to his being honoured in Huntingdonshire rather than as being the patron of a parish in Cornwall, since in the Exeter Martyrology, which has affinities with this litany, he appears as the saint of Ernulph's Bury, now Eynesbury or St Neot's in Huntingdonshire (*in uico qui dicitur ernuluesbr.*), and Cornwall is not mentioned. There seems to be observable in this ancient Exeter litany a tendency to group saints together according to the places where they were honoured. In the middle of the list of confessors comes a little group of four Celtic saints, Petroc, Gerontius, Kyeran and Cadoc, two of whom (Petroc and Kyeran) were patrons of

[13] On September 25 in the Peniarth MSS., the Mostyn MS., the Llanstephan MS., Allwydd Paradwys, and in the Primers of 1546, 1618 and 1633; on September 26 in Jesus College MS. 141 and Additional MS. 14, 882. The Mostyn MS. 88 commemorates him on February 14, which is the festival of an Irish saint of similar name, S. Manchan or Manachan, of Mohill: the Llanstephan MS. 117 on April 24; the Demetian Calendar (as Bishop and Confessor) on November 15; and the Llanstephan MS. 181 on November 18, with a note "ffair gapel feygan" (L.B.S., iii, 480). Cf. notes 3 and 5.

[14] See *The Leofric Collectar* i. 434-442, with facsimile XVII (Henry Bradshaw Society, 1914).

churches in the city of Exeter. Near the end of the list of confessors comes a second group:

SANCTE NEOTE
SANCTE WINUUALOE
SANCTE MAUCANNE
SANCTE GILDA ora.

S. Sativola and S. Welvela come at the end of the list of virgins.

It is not easy to see why a saint whose liturgical cult seems to have been so restricted as was that of S. Maucannus should appear in this litany, while much more famous saints (such as S. Samson) are omitted. It may have been due to Breton influence, since his name comes between those two very well-known Breton saints, the second of whom is not honoured with a cult anywhere on this side of the Channel. On the other hand, there is another possible explanation. Lanherne belonged to the bishops of Exeter at the time when this litany was composed. Now three other saints here invoked are apparently saints honoured in places forming part of episcopal manors. S. Cadoc's chapel and well at Padstow were on land which "belonged to the Episcopal Peculiar Deanery and Manor of Pawton" (C. G. Henderson). S. Gerontius is probably the patron of Gerrans, which "lay wholly within the great episcopal fief of Tregear" (*Cornish Church Guide*, p. 100). "King Gerentius" appears in the Exeter Martyrology as connected with S. Berriona, the eponym of Buryan and also of Veryan (the latter adjoining Gerrans); while S. Welvela must be the patron of Gulval (*Sancta Welvela de Laneskly* 1301) which, as Domesday tells us, was held by Bishop Leofric (who probably compiled this litany) before the Norman conquest.

This is the only evidence of any liturgical cult of S. Mawgan in the diocese of Exeter.[15] He is not mentioned in the Exeter Martyrology, nor in any other martyrology or litany.

Finally we must examine the references to S. Mawgan in the lives of other Celtic saints, and in medieval Welsh literature.

Rhigyfarch begins his famous Life of S. David with the story of a dream of David's father, Sant. Sant, who exercised "royal power over the people of Ceredigion, which subsequently he laid aside to procure a heavenly kingdom, was warned in dreams

[15] Strictly speaking, a litany, by itself, is not properly evidence of a *liturgical* cult of a saint in the diocese where it was compiled.

by an angelic voice, which he heard, 'Tomorrow on waking thou shalt go hunting, and having killed a stag near the river, thou shalt find there three gifts by the river Teivi, namely, the stag which thou pursuest, a fish, and a swarm of bees settled in a tree in the place which is called Llyn Henllan. Of these three, therefore, reserve a honeycomb, a part of the fish, and of the stag, which send to be kept for a son, who shall be born to thee, to the monastery of Maucannus', which till now is called the monastery of the Deposit." The symbolism of the three gifts is then explained as typifying the future career of S. David. Mr A. W. Wade-Evans identifies this Monastery of Maucannus with *Llanfeugan* in Kemes, about which the reader has heard already.

The next incident in the Life of S. David is the story of S. Patrick sailing from Demetia to convert Ireland, "having prepared a ship in Porth Mawr" close to St Davids. This, with five other legends taken from the Life of S. David, was painted in 1676 on the ceiling of the church of Saint-Divy-la-Forêt near Landerneau in Brittany, with a French inscription underneath saying that Patrick "embarks at Porth Maugan," while the words "Portus Maugan" are written over the town in the picture. The artist clearly had Rhigyfarch's Life in front of him as he worked, and that Life says *Porth Mawr*, but it is remarkable that there is a creek to the north-west of Porth Mawr called *Porth Melgan* (pronounced *Milgan*), and the artist may have known this. The whole question of the "Monasterium Maucanni" and Porth Melgan is discussed at length by Mr Wade-Evans in his edition of Rhigyfarch's work.[16]

Our study of Cornish and Breton topography has already showed us that S. Maugan is associated with S. Cadoc, places called after these saints being found close to each other. It is significant therefore that the *Vita Cadoci* introduces a *Maucan* as a character in the story of its hero. In chapter 65, which is entitled "Of King Maelgon being deprived of sight," we read that the King of Gwynedd rejected the mediation of S. Cadoc in a dispute which had arisen between him and the people of Gwynllwg. "And on that very night it was revealed by an angel to the holy man Moucam that he should restrain the king from his cruelty; who also declared to the king what had been made known to him by the angelic oracle. But he altogether

[16] S.P.C.K., 1923. I have followed Mr Wade-Evans's translation.

despised his admonitions; for early in the morning the king moved his camp to commit slaughter, and immediately he was deprived of his sight. . . . He therefore sent his messengers, namely Maucan and Argantbad, to S. Cadoc, informing him of what had happened to him, and earnestly entreated him that he would deign to visit him, and restore to him his sight." It is not clear whether *Moucam* is the same person as *Maucan*. The Life of S. Cadoc is, like all the Welsh lives of saints, very late, and of little direct historical value, but I think we may accept it in this case as proof that Welsh tradition connected S. Maugan with S. Cadoc.

The Life of S. Enda makes this very famous Irish saint go to Britain to be taught by *Maucenus*. Enda is said to have been converted by his sister Faenche, who was a nun. After his conversion his sister said to him: " 'Get thee out of thy country, and from thy kindred,' lest haply thou look back at the vanities of the world and forsake the yoke of the service of God; and go into Britain to the monastery of Rosnat, and there become a humble disciple of Maucenus, the master of that monastery. . . . Then Enda, wishing to fulfil the commands of the holy virgin, crossed the sea and came to the aforesaid Maucenus, and remained in that monastery under his direction. And after he had profited both in life and learning from the teaching there, he crossed the sea and arrived at Rome."

We must not attempt to base too much on this passage. The *Vita Endei*, as I have pointed out in my study of S. Cuby, is very late and untrustworthy; some parts of it are so wildly improbable that the Bollandists refused to print them, and the reference to S. Enda having been a disciple of S. Maucenus cannot be made to prove more than that the author had heard of S. Maugan as the abbot of a monastery in Britain and a famous teacher—a master—and so sends his hero to study at his school, as Wrdisten sends S. Winwaloe to the island of Laurea where was the monastery of S. Budoc, "a certain angelic teacher, . . . richly endowed with learning, conspicuous for righteousness, whom all people of that time regarded as a bulwark of the faith and a most firm pillar of the Church." *Rosnat* is Whithern in Galloway, but the evidence of such a worthless source as the *Vita Endei* is not enough to prove that Maugan was really abbot of Whithern, still less that we are to identify him with S. Ninian, as some have done! The apostle of Scotland had enough to occupy him there without undertaking the foundation of a very large number of churches in Wales, Cornwall and Brittany as well. It is possible that the author of the *Vita Endei* may have meant to say *Vallis Rosina* instead of Rosnat: St Davids is on the way from Ireland to Rome, while Whithern is not.

In the middle of the twelfth century Maugan is adopted by Geoffrey of Monmouth to fill a rôle in his historical romance *The Histories of the Kings of Britain*. In Book VI, c. xvii he begins the story of Merlin, which he had already treated in a separate work—it was he indeed who introduced this important element into the Arthurian legend. The mother of Merlin relates to Vortigern the strange story of the paternity of her son. "Amazed at her words, the king commanded that Maugantius should be called unto him to declare whether such a thing might be as the lady had said." Not a word is said to explain to us who Maugantius was. Geoffrey continues, "Maugantius was brought accordingly, and when he had heard the story from first to last, said unto Vortigern: 'In the books of our wise men and in many histories have I found that many men have been born into this world on this wise. For, as Apuleius . . . doth make report, certain spirits there be betwixt the moon and the earth, the which we call incubus daemons. . . . Haply one of these hath appeared unto this lady, and is the father of the youth."

It is clear that the true story of Mawgan's career has by this time been entirely forgotten. He has become a shadowy figure of the past in Welsh tradition; dimly remembered as a wise and revered teacher, he has come to be regarded as an oracle of almost supernatural wisdom, just as in the folklore of the middle ages Vergil appears as a skilled magician. Later on in Geoffrey's book (IX, xv) we read that "the bishopric of Silchester was assigned [by Arthur] to *Mauganius*," but again we are not told who Mauganius was.

The result, then, of our researches would seem to lead us to the conclusion that Maugan[17] or Malgand was an abbot, probably

[17] The reader will have observed that in Welsh literature and hagiography the name is always spelt with an *a*, and never with an *e*, while in Welsh topography *Meugan* seems universal. Mr R. Morton Nance writes: "In Welsh AU becomes modified to EU so readily that this is not surprising. Welsh DAU (=two) remains DAU in some compounds, like *daudroediog* (=biped), but becomes DEU in most of them, as *deubennog* (= two-headed), etc. '*Dehau*' and '*deheu*' are both used for 'south,' but all compounds have *eu*, as *deheubarth*. *Cau* =hollow, but *ceuedd* =cavity; *caul* =rennet, but *ceuleden* =curd, etc. So *Meugan* is perhaps due only to the presence of some other word before it—Porth, Capel, etc.—which by taking some stress off *Maugan* has affected its vowel."

an abbot-bishop, of an important monastery in Demetia, the modern Pembrokeshire, and that he shared with S. Brioc and S. Cadoc and other saints of South Wales[18] in the great movement of monastic expansion and missionary enterprise which began in the sixth century and covered Wales, Cornwall and Brittany with churches and monasteries.

[18] The saints of the Newquay district, as I have shown in my *Saint Carantoc*, seem all to have come from Pembrokeshire and Cardiganshire, and many of them are found in north-western Brittany.

SAINT CORENTIN*

PATRON OF CURY

THE legend of S. Corentin tells us nothing whatever about his parentage or early life, except that he was born of Christian parents in Armorica, and that he chose a hermit's life at Plomodiern in the forest of Nevet.

There are few more lovely views in the world than that of the bay of Douarnenez. As you stand at Douarnenez and look northwards across the blue waters of the bay, you see in front of you the cliffs of the long peninsula of Crozon (on the other side of which is the abbey of Landévennec) stretching westwards towards Brest. To the right of you rise the three peaks of the beautiful mountain called the Menez Hom.[1]

You have half Cornouaille before you, and between you and the lofty Menez Hom is the site of the hermitage of S. Corentin. "A spacious chapel, built in the form of a cross, covers the spot where his cell stood. In its gothic windows are the remains of ancient stained glass. Behind the high altar is a carved reredos on which is represented the saint being consecrated bishop. The chapel is shaded by noble trees, whose foliage hides from view the surrounding country. A few steps away is a fountain covered with a granite arch; it is on a little slope, and the stream which flows from it falls in a cascade, whose murmur is the only sound which breaks the solitude—except when the wind blows from the sea, and you hear the roar of the waves in the bay of Douarnenez, which is close by, though out of sight. The spring is the most abundant in the whole country, with the exception of that of Sainte-Candide at Scaër" (*Saint Corentin*, by Abbé A. Thomas).

In this fountain, or in the stream flowing from it, we are told, there lived a miraculous fish. Each day S. Corentin cut from it a slice to serve for his daily meal, and the instant he replaced it in the water the fish was whole as before. It came to pass that one day Grallon, king of Cornouaille, was hunting in the forest and

* Cornish Saints Series, no. 5 (1925), being a sermon preached in Cury parish-church on 9 August 1925.

[1] The "authorities" followed by the author of *The Churches and Antiquities of Cury and Gunwalloe* have led him into some strange blunders, among others that of identifying the Menez Hom with Menheniot!

found S. Corentin by the sacred fountain. The king and his courtiers were tired and hungry, and asked for food. Corentin undertook to feed the party, and going to the fountain he cut from his fish sufficient to satisfy the wants of all. The courtiers were stupefied and one of them, out of curiosity, took the fish himself and cut a piece from it—but it was now bleeding and mutilated. Corentin healed the fish and warned it to disappear to avoid further ill-treatment, and it was never seen again. To show his gratitude, King Grallon gave Corentin his property in the neighbouring forest and a hunting seat it contained. (Down to 1789 Plomodiern belonged to the bishops of Quimper.)

One day Corentin left Plomodiern to visit another hermit in the forest of Nevet, S. Primel, or Primaël. (Readers of Anatole Le Braz will remember his description of S. Primel in *The Land of Pardons*, ii, c. 1.) The site of his hermitage is marked by a ruined chapel in the parish of Saint-Thois (and the visit of Corentin to Primel is the subject of one of the paintings by Yan Dargent in the cathedral of Quimper). After a day spent in conversation about sacred things, the night was passed by the two holy men in psalms and hymns and spiritual songs. In the morning they prepared to celebrate the Holy Mysteries. Water was wanted to mix with the altar wine; Primel departed to fetch some. The well was distant, and Primel was old and lame. Moved with compassion, Corentin struck the ground near the oratory with his staff, and a copious spring gushed forth. (This incident is probably introduced on account of the fact that a chapel of S. Primel existed in Quimper, the city of Corentin.) The report of these miracles soon brought to Corentin's hermitage two saintly visitors, Patern and Malo. Corentin gave them a welcome and offered them hospitality; he had nothing in his cell except a little bread, but going with his pitcher to the fountain to fetch water he found it full of eels, which he cooked and set before his guests. The water in the jug, too, had become wine. Patern and Malo returned home full of wonder at what had happened, praising him who "openeth his hand and filleth all things living with plenteousness."

At length, the people of Cornouaille demanded Corentin to be their first bishop. Nothing is told us with regard to this extremely interesting and important step of the creation of the new diocese of Cornouaille, about which we should be so glad to be informed. Nor are we told by whom Corentin had been ordained priest.

He was sent to Tours to be consecrated by S. Martin, in company with two monks conspicuous for wisdom and holiness, S. Winwaloe and S. Tudy. S. Martin laid his hands on him and hallowed him bishop, but when asked to bless Winwaloe and Tudy as abbots of two monasteries in Cornouaille he refused, saying that that was the office of Corentin as their diocesan, and that if *he* did so, it might be a precedent to his successors to claim it as a right, to the prejudice of the bishops of Cornouaille. The Sanctoral of Quimper of 1500 states that Grallon sent Corentin, Winwaloe and Tudy to Martin asking him to consecrate whichever of the three he thought most fit for the office.

Corentin returned to his diocese and was received with great honour. He blessed Winwaloe and Tudy, and installed them, presumably at Landévennec and Loctudy. He diligently watched over the flock committed to him, and proved a shining example of every virtue (in painful contrast, says the anonymous author of the oldest Life of S. Corentin, with too many of his successors at Quimper). By his preaching he converted wicked men, unbelievers and apostate Christians, and brought back many erring souls to the fold of the Church. At length, worn out with his labours, he restored to Christ the talent committed to his keeping and departed to the joys of Heaven. After his death many miracles made his name a household word in Brittany. He was succeeded by S. Conogan.

§

Such is the legend of S. Corentin. Legend is history, in the sense that the legends and traditions of a people are part of its history. Everyone who learns the history of Rome is told the story of Romulus and Remus. No one would know Brittany who did not know its legends and its folk-lore. From these legends we learn that the soul of the Breton people was moulded at its birth by the saints of the fifth and sixth centuries. "The delicate tone of pure and sincere enthusiasm which characterizes the Breton and Irish legends of the saints," said no less a person than Renan, "is truly wonderful, and no church has anything to compare with it."[2]

[2] I would mention the reference to the Breton saints, especially SS. Winwaloe and Corentin, in ch. 4 of René Bazin's charming Breton novel *Madame Corentine*.

But criticism must rigorously examine and test in each case the stories handed down about the early Breton saints. What has criticism to say with regard to the legend of S. Corentin?

It is clear that the author of the manuscript Life I have paraphrased lived after the primatial dignity of Dol had been abolished and Brittany had become once more part of the ecclesiastical province of Tours. No Breton writer earlier than the twelfth century would have represented S. Corentin as having been consecrated by S. Martin, which in itself is of course impossible, as Martin died before the immigration from Britain into Armorica had begun. The Life of Corentin that this old writer has left us contains very little, if any, trustworthy information about him. But one thing I think we may learn from the legends it records. S. Corentin was a hermit. The most characteristic feature about the Celtic church was its preference for the monastic and eremitic life. It is quite what we should expect to find when we are told that the first bishop of Quimper was taken from a hermitage (the Life of S. Petroc shows us SS. Samson and Guethnoc, already bishops, living in cells by themselves). A curious example in our own time of a hermit of the Celtic type may be found in Charles de Foucauld at Beni Abbès in the Sahara. René Bazin relates how Brother Charles's enclosure was respected: "His reputation for holiness made everything within it sacred. The nomad unloaded his camel inside the row of stones which marked its boundaries, the poor Arab woman left her fagot there, the butcher deposited his pile of blood-stained goatskins, sure to find them there next day unmolested." Bazin's most interesting biography also shows how legends grow up about remarkable characters even during their lifetime: "Already legend had taken possession of the story of the hermit of Nazareth and Jerusalem, and embellished it with its ornaments, often groundless and false. The villagers related that Brother Charles loved to let himself down to the bottom of a dry well, there to pray undisturbed for hours. Nothing was true in these and similar stories, except the veneration which created them."

Further, it is very significant that the bishops of Quimper down to the time of the Revolution were not entitled "of Quimper" but "of Cornouaille," the diocese was called the diocese of Cornouaille and the canons of Quimper cathedral were canons of Cornouaille. Contrary to the universal custom of the Western church, the bishop of this Breton see took his title, not from a city, but from a district, a district the name of which, identical with that of a modern English county, shows it to have been a colony from the south-western extremity of Great Britain. It is just possible that the see city of Cornouaille may have been originally Carhaix, which was certainly the capital of the district in Roman times; but it is probable that Corentin lived at Quimper, as there is a holy well there bearing his name (on the south side of the river Odet, in the Rue Pont-Firmin), the cathedral is dedicated to our Lady and S. Corentin, and Quimper was known as Quimper-Corentin down to the Revolution. He is also the patron of Poullaouen and at Baud.

The first mention of S. Corentin in history is found in Wrdisten's Life of S. Winwaloe (*q.v.*), where a verse of poetry associates the names of Winwaloe, Grallon and Corentin, and says they lived after the time of S. Tudual, founder of Tréguier. These three names were clearly the names handed down by tradition as those of the three chief figures in the early history of Cornouaille—the king[3] or count of Cornouaille, the first bishop, and the founder of Landévennec. Several counts of Cornouaille in historical times bore the name of Grallon, and it is significant that all through the tenth and eleventh centuries the counts and bishops of Cornouaille were closely connected, the bishop being always chosen from the family of the count (for some time the bishopric was hereditary).

The next references to S. Corentin are found in ancient litanies. In the very old one known as the Litany of Saint-Vougay, at the head of a long list of Breton saints whose prayers are invoked, come the names of the founders of the sees of Dol (S. Samson), of Saint-Malo and Saint-Brieuc, S. Guidgal, S. Melaine of Rennes, S. Patern of Vannes and finally S. Corentin (spelt *Sce Chourentine*. J. Loth says that *Cowrentin* would be the original form of the name), followed immediately by S. Winwaloe. S. Corentin's name is found in the canon of the Mass in a Winchester missal of the tenth century (Corpus Christi College,

[3] There was in the seventeenth century a kind of cult of King Grallon. Albert Le Grand tells us that in his time the parishes near Landévennec, as Argol, Dineol, Saint-Nic, etc., used on certain days to go to the abbey and sing a service in the oratory of King Grallon for the repose of his soul. Down to the Revolution it was the custom on S. Cecilia's day for the clergy to go up to the statue of Grallon between the two western towers of Quimper cathedral, where a hymn was sung with orchestral accompaniment. A man then climbed on to the statue with a glass of wine and a napkin; he offered the glass to the king, drank it himself, wiped the king's lips and tossed the goblet to the crowd below. If anyone caught it unbroken he was rewarded with 100 crowns, but the reward is believed never to have been claimed.

Cambridge) and in the litany of a psalter of Tours used at Christ Church, Canterbury, in the eleventh century. In the twelfth century, the abbey of Abingdon claimed to possess a bone of *S. Caurentin.*

S. Corentin is mentioned in the *Roman d'Aquin*, in the second half of the twelfth century (Édition Jouon des Longrais, vv. 2023-3040, and note p. 178).

§

I have said that, in a certain sense, legend is history. The cult of the saints is also history, and we find the cult of S. Corentin in Brittany all through the middle ages. A favourite Breton medieval devotion was that known as *Tro Breiz*, the pilgrimage made four times a year to the shrines of the Seven Saints of Brittany, the founders of the sees of Dol, Saint-Malo, Saint-Brieuc, Tréguier, Saint-Pol-de-Léon, Cornouaille and Vannes. S. Corentin was one of the seven. A sequence used on his festival began:

Septem sanctos veneremur
Et in illis admiremur
Septiformem gratiam

His praefulsit Corentinus,
Consecravit quem Martinus
Praesulem Cornubiae.

The author of the oldest Life of the saint tells us that owing to the miracles wrought at Quimper they had had to pull down the cathedral and build a larger one. In 1018 Alain Caignard, the count of Cornouaille, feared he was going blind. At the instance of his wife Judicaël, he had himself carried to the cathedral of Quimper, and after praying there and offering at the altar a charter giving to God and S. Corentin certain lands, he found his sight completely restored. Two young men of the House of Cornouaille were saved from sickness and death by the prayers of S. Corentin. A woman who intended to offer several ounces of wax at his shrine changed her mind at the last moment, but found that she could no longer open the hand she had closed to withdraw the offering; on her repentance Corentin appeared to her in a dream and healed her. A thief from Léon who stole some silk at the Pardon of S. Corentin on May 1 was struck with fever and palsy, but was healed by the saint on his repentance. The abbey of Marmoutier near Tours, where the body of S. Corentin was carried during the Norman invasion of the tenth century and retained by the monks, who were very proud of it, was one day visited by brigands, who broached a large cask containing the monks' winter store of wine. After other relics had been tried without effect, those of S. Corentin were brought, when the wine immediately ceased to flow out of the cask and the brigands departed in consternation. Such were the stories of wonders due to S. Corentin's intercession told round the fireside by Quimper men in an uncritical age.

The miracle of the fish will recall to every Cornishman the story in the life of S. Neot, represented in one of the ancient glass windows of his church in East Cornwall. It occurs again in the Life of S. Petroc. (It has been suggested that the miraculous fish is derived from a heathen Irish myth—the "Salmon of Science" that lived in "the fountain of Coppla".)

The cult of S. Corentin received an extraordinary impetus in the seventeenth century, which saw a great religious revival all over France, and especially in Brittany. If in Brittany it did not leave the wonderful literary monuments—sermons like those of Bossuet, books of devotion like those of S. Francis de Sales—it produced in other parts of France, it left a no less lasting monument in the intense and permanent devotion to the Catholic religion that it aroused in the entire Breton peasantry. The leader of the religious revival in Brittany was Father Julian Maunoir, a Jesuit, "the John Wesley of Brittany."[4] It was through the influence of another Jesuit, Father Bernard, of Quimper, that Maunoir was called to this work. In 1639 and 1640 the plague visited Quimper, and a third of the inhabitants died. In obedience to what he believed to be a supernatural admonition, Father Bernard called the citizens together and they made a vow to erect a screen in the cathedral and place there the relic of the arm of S. Corentin, recently recovered from Marmoutier by the bishop of Cornouaille. The fountain of S. Corentin was restored and the broken image of the saint beneath the shrine that covered it was replaced by a new statue; the old one was repaired and set up in the Jesuit college. The plague then ceased. In the same year Maunoir began the Breton missions, in which he was to labour for forty-three years. S. Corentin was Maunoir's favourite saint. Among the Breton hymns he wrote to sing during his missions (another parallel with the Methodist movement in Cornwall) was a metrical Life of S. Corentin. There is also a Breton hymn to the saint by Michel Le Nobletz, the precursor of Maunoir. During

[4] [Maunoir was beatified at Rome in 1951.—*Editor.*]

this period there lived in Quimper a girl called Catherine Daniélou, who was closely associated with those engaged in the work of the Breton missions. She had been driven from home by an unnatural mother and a brutal stepfather, and the story of her life is a succession of visions and supernatural events. She was told to take S. Corentin in the place of her father, and we are told the saint constantly appeared to her and befriended her.

In the middle ages the chief festival of S. Corentin was on May 1. At the present time it is on December 12. At 5 a.m. the bells of Quimper cathedral sound and the church is immediately invaded by crowds of pilgrims from all parts of Cornouaille (a crowd of peasants who have walked fifteen miles and more to church in dark and cold and pouring rain is a sight more frequently seen in Brittany than in England). At the Mass there is a sermon on S. Corentin in Breton, and Breton hymns are sung. *Cornics* are a special feature of the feast of S. Corentin, as eggs are of Easter. They are little cakes of oatmeal, shaped like a mitre and slightly raised in the centre, which is gilded. They are bought at S. Corentin's fair and sent to absent friends. The custom is first mentioned only in 1790, but it is much older.

The church of Cury in Cornwall is dedicated in honour of S. Corentin. It is *Capella Sti Corentini* in Bishop Stapeldon's Register. During the middle ages the parish was dependent on that of Breage. In 1890 a fresco was discovered in Breage church, representing S. Corentin in cope, dalmatic and alb, with a massive pastoral staff and a very large mitre. By his side is the legendary fish, and above his head in black letter are the words "Ste quorentine ora pro nobis".

Mr C. G. Henderson writes in a letter to me dated 10 July [1925]: "Cury is sometimes called Egloskerry in old deeds and sometimes Curriton, i.e. Corentin. I don't think however that Egloskerry near Launceston is the same saint, for in the fifteenth century the dedication is given to St Keria, Virgin, one of Brychan's children. There is no doubt that Cury is S. Corentin, and that there was a Celtic monastery there, as the name Lamana (Lan-manach) would imply. Lamana is near Cury church. The subjection to Breage was probably only a post-Conquest arrangement, due to the fact that the manor of Winnianton extended into Breage."

I end with a few fragments from hymns in honour of S. Corentin, in Latin, Breton and French.

Pange solemnes, pia turba, cantus
Hac die cunctis tibi sanctiori
Quae Corentinum cumulata palmis
  Vexit ad astra.

Carne dum piscis redit integrata
In cibum sese toties daturus
Aequa lex strictae quoties suadet
  Prandia mensae.

Sant Corentin, patron Kerne,
Diouallit mad hor bro;
Grit ma virimp lezen Doue
Beteg heur ar maro.

Holy Corentin, patron of Cornouaille,
Defend our land well;
Enable us to keep God's law
Unto our lives' end.

E Kerne, menez ha traonien
Zo deoc'h a berz Doue;
Glepet int bet gant ho c'houezen
Dalc'hit stard d'ho leve.

In Cornouaille, mountain and valley
Are yours on God's behalf;
They have been watered by your sweat,
Hold fast to your revenue.

O peuple de Cornouaille,
  Célebre ton pasteur!
Sol du Léon tressaille,
  Pour l'élu du Seigneur.
Que nos bourgs et nos villes
  Chantent saint Corentin,
Sur les flots, dans les îles
  Exaltez-le sans fin!

SAINT KEVERNE*

Patron of St Keverne

NEAR the Lizard is a parish now called St Keverne; this saint, like S. Perran, has been wrongly identified with the Irish S. Ciarán of Saighir through the well-meaning attentions of ignorant hagiographers. [In the course of his account of the parish and its dedication in Cornish Saints Series no. 29, Charles Henderson gives the following information:]

The north-eastern half of the Lizard peninsula, comprising the parishes of Mawgan, St Martin, Manaccan, St Anthony and St Keverne, has, for the last 1000 years at least and probably for a considerable time longer, gone by the popular name of Meneage, pronounced Menāgue. This name, like Roseland, has no official significance. It is the name of neither a hundred, a rural deanery nor an honour, yet it has held its ground from a period earlier than any of those institutions in Cornwall. The word Meneage is thought to be connected with *Manach*, a monk, and to imply the "monkish land."[1] This is by no means certain, although it is clear that in Celtic times there were a number of small monasteries in the area.

Lesneague in St Keverne, anciently *Lesmanaoc* (967), *Lismanahec* (1150) etc., was, from its name, the capital (*Lis*=Court) of the region. We find it the chief house on some territory bestowed upon the monks of St Michael's Mount by the Count of Mortain *circa* 1080.

St Keverne, however, is one of the largest parishes in Cornwall, and its church, with the land-owning monastery belonging to it, whose lands are now called Lanheverne, seems to have been independent of Lesmeneague.

According to the Geld Inquest of 1083 the canons of *S. Achebranus*[2] held one hide of land in the hundred of *Winningtone* (Kerrier) which never paid geld, a proof of its ancient ecclesiastical ownership. In Domesday (1085) this is more fully described. Here

* From Cornish Saints Series, no. 29, *Saint Perran, Saint Keverne and Saint Kerrian* (1931)

[1] Manacles Point near St Keverne is clearly a corruption of Meneage-als, *i.e.* Meneage Cliff.

[2] Although *Kieran* and *Kyran* became the official spellings of the church's name during the fourteenth and fifteenth centuries, the older *Achebran* or *Akeveran* held its ground in popular speech and returned as *Keverne* at the Reformation. *Kieran* can never have been a genuine form of the name.

we are told that the lands held by the canons of *S. Achebrannus* in *Lannachebran* had been seized by the Count of Mortain, whose robbery of church property in Cornwall has been noticed in the account of Perran-zabulo. . . .

. . . The attempt of the medieval ecclesiastics to identify the patron of St Keverne with Kieran or Piran is not borne out by the earliest spellings of the name, S. *Ach*[3]*ebrann* (1085), *Akeveran* (1201), *Akevran* (1278), *Kaveran* (1235), etc. or by the present pronunciation Keverne. The form *Kyeran* does not seem to occur much before 1283, certainly not before the place fell into the hands of the Cistercian monks of Beaulieu who were, perhaps, responsible for the attempt to identify the name with the Irish *Ciarán*. Southern Ireland was peculiarly rich in Cistercian monasteries, so that the name of Ciarán would have been well known to members of the order in the British Isles.

Akeveran is probably the truest form of the name of the patron saint of St Keverne. Compounded with Lan the name becomes Lanheverne, which is still applied to part of the church-town. Trehaverne in Kenwyn, the *Tregavran* of Domesday, Tregaverne near Port Isaac in North Cornwall, and possibly Goon-haverne in Perran-zabulo, may contain the personal name, but the latter is spelt *Goenhavar* in 1290 and may simply be the "Summer pasture down," or the "Goat's down."

According to a well-known legend, S. Just after visiting S. Keverne absconded with his chalice. His host threw three rocks at the thief as he was going westwards. These fell in a field near the road from Helston to Marazion, not far from Germoe, and were known as Tremenheverne or the Three Stones of Keverne. They were supposed to be unlike any rock found in the Germoe district but similar to the stones found on Crowza downs in St Keverne. Such is the story as related by Hunt and other late collectors of Cornish legends. On the Germoe parish map (1840) the field in question, part of Hallegan tenement, is given the name of *Menheveren* or *Menherveren*. This name certainly suggests the meaning "Stone of Keverne." It would be interesting to trace it further back.

[After referring the reader to Mr Henderson's study, Canon Doble goes on:] I would only add here a few lines in order that the reader may know what Joseph Loth has written on this saint

[3] The *Ch* in Domesday is intended to represent *K*.

in the article I have already referred to [in the *Mémoires de la Société d'Histoire et d'Archéologie de Bretagne*, 1930, pp. 157 *et seq*].

He points out that *Keverne* is a corruption of an earlier *Kevran*. The *v* was soon followed by an "*e* of resonance," and *Keveran* quickly became *Kevern* according to a well-known law in which vowel and consonant in Cornish so frequently get transposed. Loth gives as an example the Middle-Cornish *ebren* (=heaven) which in modern Cornish is *ebbarn*, and the reader may recall many other examples from Cornish place-names.[4] The form of the name in Domesday, *Achebran*, he considers to have been a blunder of the canons there, who turned *Lanna-Kebran* into *Lan-Achebran*. (Lampaul in Brittany was formerly Lanna-Pauli, rendered in a ninth-century manuscript as *monasteriolum Pauli*.) I would like however to point out that we have another instance in the period of Domesday of an *a* being inserted before the name of a saint. S. Neot is called in the Geld Inquest of 1083 *Sanctus Anietus*. Loth comments caustically on the attempt of the authors of the *Lives of the British Saints* to identify Achebran with an Irish saint Aed Cobran. At the same time he thinks that *kevran* and *kebran* are derived from an old Cornish root *cobran*, which means *one who helps*. *Cobrant* appears frequently in the cartulary of Redon. Later it was pronounced *covrant*, and from it is derived the name of the famous Armorican saint Corentin.

Saint Kerrian

We have seen that two different Cornish saints, Perran and Keverne, have been sacrificed to increase the glory of an Irish saint. I think it is clear that a third Dumnonian saint has suffered the same fate. At Exeter there was formerly a church of *S. Kerian*, situated in the part of the city inhabited by the Britons up to 936, when Athelstan expelled them. The churches in this quarter are all dedicated to Celtic saints: S. David, S. Petroc, S. Paul of Léon, etc. An examination of the different spellings of the name of the patron saint of S. Kerian's will show that at Exeter, as at Perran-zabulo, there was a tendency to alter the name to make it appear more like *Kyaran*. In the Episcopal Registers in 1310, 1312, 1332, and 1362 it is *Ecclesia Sti Kerani*, in

[4] Thus *Cambron* has become *Camborne*.

1399 and 1408 *Kerani* and *Kierani*, in 1438 *Kierani*, in 1440 *Kerani*, in 1441 *Kierani*. *Keriani* is found in the fifteenth century and Hogenberg's map of Exeter in 1527 shows the church of *S. Keriane*.[5]

If S. Ciarán were really the patron of S. Kerian's, he would be the only Irish saint honoured in Exeter. All the rest are British saints, and it would be hard to explain this solitary instance. But it is clear, I think, that S. Kerian's is called after a Dumnonian saint, who must have been an important personage, as the Celtic dedications at Exeter are nearly all to very famous people. A saint called *Kerianus* appears in Albert Le Grand's *Vie de S. Ké* as a disciple of that saint, buried by him at Cleder: and a S. Kerian is the eponym of the parish of Querrien near Quimperlé, and of the *trève* of Saint-Keran[6] in Treflaouenan. It is a common name in Brittany. There is a Kerian in Chateaulin, and a Querrien near Loudéac.

I even think that S. Kerian may *possibly* have been honoured, side by side with S. Kebran, at St Keverne in Cornwall. It is a remarkable fact that in Cornish parishes whose names begin with *Lan* the parish church is hardly ever dedicated to the saint whose name is compounded with the *Lan*. The name of the holy well at St Keverne, Funten-Keran, perhaps supports this view. The monks of Beaulieu may (as Mr Henderson suggests) have tried to identify Keverne with Ciarán, but they may have been led to do so by finding that a S. Kerian was honoured there. St Keverne is very close to Brittany, and must have been in constant communication with that country, and it is in a district full of dedications to Breton saints.[7]

[5] Mrs Frances Rose-Troup has kindly sent me the following note: "S. Kerian occurs in the Kalendar of the Leofric Psalter [Harleian MS. 863] dated 1173, as *Kerani* and in the Litany in the same as *Kyerane;* in the Ordinance of Bishop Marshall [1194—1204] as *Kerani;* in the Grant of Peter of Palerma [c. 1214] as *Kierani*. A small church dedicated to him stood in North Street, Exeter; only the tower remains and an inscription is attached 'Here stood the ancient church of S. Kerian, which, having fallen into decay, was demolished A.D. 1878.' Since the Reformation the benefice has been united with that of S. Petrock, but the parishioners still assert their independence by electing their churchwardens. In a rental of *c.* 1265 the name occurs as *Sancto Karano*, a rent of sixpence being paid to the Chapter. A tenement *versus Portam Borealem* was given by the will of John Doulis in 1257 to maintain lights in the churches of S. Keiran and S. Cuthbert." [The present tower of S. Kerian's is a quite modern structure, though the clock *may* be ancient.]

[6] In Brittany, as at Exeter, *Kerian* and *Keran*, are found as different forms of the same name. In Cornwall *Gwithian* is locally pronounced *Gwithan*.

[7] R. Largillière has shown in his *Six Saints de Plestin* that S. Garan or Haran (pronounced C'haran) is the patron of Cavan, and that Cavan and Garan are the same name. Since about 1679 S. Chéron of Chartres has been the patron of Cavan.

One thing at any rate is clear, *viz.* that neither the Exeter Kerian nor the Lizard Keverne or Kyeran (the forms *Keran* and *Keyran* are also found) can be the same as S. Ciarán, for if Piran were really the British form of Ciarán, those parishes would bear the British, not the Irish, form of the name.

SAINT WINWALOE*

Patron of Gunwalloe, Landewednack and Other Places

... The names of the two Lizard parishes of Cury and Gunwalloe are of quite extraordinary interest to the historian. They are reminders, not only of the close connection between Brittany and the south-western portion of Great Britain from which the Bretons emigrated, but of the particular connection between our Cornwall and the Cornwall in Brittany—"Armorican Cornwall." The south-western part of Brittany, of which Quimper is the capital, is known as *Cornouaille*, in Latin Cornubia or Cornugallia, and it is so called because it was colonized from Cornwall. Now the parishes of Cury and Gunwalloe take their names from the two chief saints of Cornouaille, SS. Corentin and Winwaloe, honoured respectively at Quimper and Landévennec. Additional interest arises from the fact that close to Cury and Gunwalloe is *Landewednack*, and the Armorican abbey of *Landévennec* was originally the chief religious centre of Cornouaille.

Landewednack (*Landewennec* in 1310) is the same name as Landévennec, and the church in both places was dedicated in honour of Saint Winwaloe (an alternative name for Landewednack, frequently found in old deeds, was "Gonwallo in Lizard"). There is perhaps nowhere else in Cornwall clearer evidence of the constant intercourse which must once have existed between the two countries.

Saint Winwaloe is, then, patron of two churches in the south of Cornwall. He is also patron of Tremaine in the north. Before the Reformation there were two other Cornish parishes containing chapels dedicated to him, and he is still patron of a parish close by on the south coast of Devon. On the other side of the Channel we find that he is one of the best-known of all the Breton saints, with a very widespread cult, especially in Finistère. He was the founder and patron saint of one of the leading abbeys in Brittany.

In Brittany, as in all other Celtic countries, the ecclesiastical organization was largely monastic. If we had visited Brittany in

* Cornish Saints Series, no. 4 (2nd edn., 1940).

the period between the fifth and tenth centuries, we should have found a number of large monasteries, often with bishops residing in them or ruling over them, five of which later became the seats of the dioceses of Dol, Saint-Malo, Saint-Brieuc, Tréguier and Saint-Pol-de-Léon, while others adopted the Rule of S. Benedict and became abbeys of the usual Western type; and together with these we should have found a great many smaller monasteries, which eventually, as in Wales and Cornwall, became parish churches. In the church of each monastery the founder was buried, and his bell, cross, staff and gospel-book were kept on his tomb as relics.

In the tenth century a great disaster befell Brittany. The Norsemen conquered the country in 914 and occupied it till 939. When it became certain that every monastery would be sacked, the monks fled into the interior of France, taking with them their chief treasures, including the body of their saintly founder and (in many cases) his written Life—anyone who reads, *e.g.*, the *Vita Guduali*, composed in the abbey of Blandinium at Ghent, will see that it is based on a Life brought with the saint's body from Locoal.

One of the most important monasteries in Brittany was at Landévennec in Cornouaille. When, however, at a period and in circumstances unknown to us, a diocese of Cornouaille was established, the church of Quimper was chosen to be the cathedral, though Landévennec remained one of the most considerable religious communities in the new diocese and S. Winwaloe one of its chief saints. It had been generously endowed with gifts of land all over Léon and Cornouaille, but at the beginning of the ninth century it did not own more than about half of what we find it possessing two centuries later. The abbey emerges definitely into the clear light of history in the year 818, when Louis the Pious, at war with Morvan, appeared at the head of an army in the valley of Ellé. The Carolingian emperors endeavoured, like the Saxon kings of England, to abolish the peculiar Celtic usages in the churches of countries under their control. When the abbot of Landévennec, Matmonoc, visited Louis in his camp, the emperor was shocked to see his Celtic tonsure. The Rule of S. Benedict was in consequence introduced, by his order, at Landévennec, though this does not mean that the monastery was refounded.

In the middle of the ninth century Landévennec was in a very flourishing condition. Its abbot for about thirty years or more in the second half of that century[1] was a monk of literary tastes, named Wrdisten (or Gourdisten), who wrote poetry as well as prose. He composed more than one Life of the founder of the abbey, and from these are derived every account of S. Winwaloe that we possess.

In 914 the monks of Landévennec had to leave their monastery, which was burnt by the Norsemen. They took with them the body of S. Winwaloe, his bell, his chasuble, and other similar relics, and his written Life, and made their way first, it seems, to Château-du-Loir, half-way between Le Mans and Tours. The interesting church of this little town is still dedicated to S. *Guingalois*, and one of the two chief manuscripts of Wrdisten's Life of S. Winwaloe was written (or at any rate preserved) here.[2] From Château-du-Loir, where they made only a short stay, the monks went on to Montreuil-sur-Mer, not far from Boulogne. At first sight we might be surprised at their choice, since Montreuil might seem quite as much exposed to raids by pirates as Landévennec, but no doubt they had heard that the brave and patriotic Helgaud, count of Ponthieu and Montreuil, had strongly fortified this town, which stands on a hill in a very commanding position and has always possessed great strategic importance, and held it against all attacks by the Normans.[3] The body of S. Winwaloe was placed in the church of the abbey of Saint-Sauve in Montreuil, and was in course of time surrounded by numerous other relics of Celtic saints placed there for safety. Within the hospitable precincts of the abbey the monastic community of Landévennec continued its corporate existence unbroken. Its abbot, John (the third abbot after Wrdisten), was a very capable

[1] Wrdisten says that the monk Clement was dead when he was writing and that he had written his hymn in honour of S. Winwaloe "in the time when Salomon ruled over the Britons." As Salomon's reign began in November 857, this helps to date Wrdisten's literary activities. Wrmonoc, the author of the *Vita Pauli Aureliani*, written in 884, tells us that he undertook this work at the suggestion of Abbot Wrdisten, who was then still living.

[2] There was a priory at Château-du-Loir, belonging to the abbey of Marmoutier. The present church possesses an eleventh-century crypt which may be part of the church of S. Winwaloe built by Hamelin, the owner of the castle, in 1030. The manuscript referred to in the text contains an interesting couple of elegiac verses, stating that:

> "Lambertus laicus equidem me scribere fecit
> Winwaloei patris eximii titulo:
> Cuius frater erat Medardus, dives in omni
> Cornubiae gaza; nec minus ille fuit."

See R. Charles, *S. Gudagalois: ses reliques, son culte et son prieuré à Château-du-Loir* (Mamers, 1879).

[3] Helgaud's predecessor Haymon had founded the abbey of Saint-Josse-sur-Mer in honour of a Celtic saint, Judocus.

and public-spirited man. He proved of great service to Alain Barbetorte, who in 939 placed himself at the head of the Breton exiles in England, collected, with the help of King Athelstan, a considerable force and, returning to Brittany, wiped out the Normans in a succession of battles. John and his monks returned to Brittany with him and rebuilt the abbey of Landévennec.

The body of S. Winwaloe, however, was not brought back from Montreuil. It remained there till it was destroyed by fanatics, together with all the other relics in the abbey church of Saint-Sauve, during the French Revolution. Montreuil became a new centre of the cult of S. Winwaloe, which from thence not only spread widely over the north of France, but was carried over into England. Thus the entry for S. Winwaloe on March 3 in the Exeter Martyrology (as revised by Bishop Grandisson) runs "*In Pikardia* deposicio sancti Wingualoci confessoris atque abbatis."[4]

The abbey of Landévennec was richly rewarded for the patriotic spirit it had shown during this crisis. Alan rebuilt Nantes and made it his capital. While doing this, he signed a charter recording his gratitude to Abbot John, who had "invited us [to come to Brittany] and had made several journeys across the sea, had acted as an intermediary in negotiations with the Saxons and the Normans, and had obtained an oath of fidelity to us before our arrival and brought the good news back, to our great joy." Consequently he grants "upon the altar of S. Peter the Apostle" in the cathedral of Nantes "to Saint Guingualoaeus and to his Abbot John" the abbey of Saint-Médard, the church of Holy Cross within the city of Nantes and the church of St Cyricus outside the city, and the whole island of Baht Wenrann (*i.e.*, Batz in Guérande, west of Nantes).[5] One of the witnesses to this charter, called Moisen, imitated Alan's generosity and gave "to Saint Winwaloaeus" a piece of land he owned in the parish of Carentoir *in pago Brouuerec* (*i.e.*, in the Vannetais).[6] Several of the counts of Cornouaille and other generous benefactors added further gifts during the hundred years or so that followed, and in the eleventh century a monk of the abbey resolved to draw up a cartulary, giving a list of all its possessions and analysing the

[4] The older version of the martyrology, contained in a twelfth-century manuscript at Exeter (Exeter Chapter MSS .3518), omits "In Pikardia." It also omits the entry "translacio sancti Wingualoci abbatis et confessoris" which the later version of the martyrology inserts on April 28.

[5] Cartulary of Landévennec, No. XXV. This charter seems to have been badly copied, and several of the sentences quoted are obscure, though their general sense seems clear.

[6] ib. No. XL.

charters granting them. Unfortunately those granted previously to 914 had been destroyed by the Normans, and he was obliged to invent charters for all the oldest estates belonging to the monastery, which he placed to the credit of a legendary King Gradlon, of whom he had read in Wrdisten's Life of S. Winwaloe. For the other possessions of the abbey he had better authority. The monks had brought back from Montreuil a charter signed there (Count Helgaud being one of the witnesses). The charters of Alain Barbetorte and Moysen already referred to had been carefully preserved, and so had all those granted since.

The cartulary is contained in a manuscript now in the Public Library at Quimper (MS. 16), which begins with a version of the completest form of Wrdisten's Life of S. Winwaloe. This occupies f. 3 to f. 126v., that is, by far the larger part of the book. It is followed by a hymn in honour of the saint for Vespers *in natali Sancti Winwaloei*, and another for Matins, and a longer alphabetical one, containing twenty-three verses, by the monk Clement to whom Wrdisten refers in his Life of Winwaloe: this, we are told, was sung at Landévennec every Sunday at Matins from All Saints to Easter, the other being used from Easter to All Saints. This section ends with a homily on the life of S. Winwaloe, also by Wrdisten, for his festival. After this comes a short Life of another saint, Ethbin, who is here identified with S. Idunet of Châteaulin: then a list of the abbots of Landévennec, the cartulary proper, a list of the counts of Cornouaille, and a few miscellaneous notes by later hands. If we add to all this the Gospel-book of the Abbey of Landévennec (Bodl. Libr., MS. Auct. D.2.16) and the kalendar used in the abbey (Royl Libr. of Copenhagen, Thott, in-fol., 239; unfortunately imperfect[7]), we shall have before us all the available sources for the early history of Cornouaille.

[7] The gospel-book and the kalendar are described by Duine in *Inventaire liturgique de l'hagiographie bretonne* (Paris, 1922), pp. 49–53. Two other copies of the gospel-book of Landévennec are known. One is the magnificent *Harkness Gospels* in the Library of the City of New York. A beautifully illustrated article on this manuscript, entitled *The Gospelbook of Landévennec*, by C. R. Morey and E. H. Kraeling, appeared in *Art Studies*, vol. viii, part ii (1931), pp. 225–286, with 40 plates (all the illuminations have been reproduced). Prof. Morey has also printed a brochure entitled *The Landévennec Gospels* (New York, 1929). The manuscript was described in 1819 as "from the Monastery of Como" (It is to be observed that Wrdisten wrote a letter to John, Bishop of Arezzo, thanking him for his kindness to two Landévennec monks.) It seems to be of the second half of the 9th century. The illuminations are of a debased Merovingian type. It is doubtful if there is any Irish influence. Prof. Morey notes "one original and native note. Birds are the stock ornament of Merovingian art, but here they invariably hold a fish in beak or talons. . . . May we not see in this a reminiscence of the gulls of the Breton coast, a motif familiar to a race of fishermen?" The other copy is in the Public Library of Berne in Switzerland (No. 85).

This bird's eye view of the whole subject will, I hope, enable the reader to follow the attempt to deal with the problems presented by the Life of S. Winwaloe. I will give an analysis of Wrdisten's Life, afterwards proceeding to a critical examination of the information it contains. But first it will be necessary to describe the differing versions of it which we possess.

We have seen that the Cartulary of Landévennec[8] contains a copy of the *Vita Sancti Winwaloei*. Another manuscript, now in the National Library at Paris (MS. lat., 5610a), but formerly at Château-du-Loir, gives us practically the same text.[9] Latouche[10] calls these two manuscripts B1 and B2 respectively. The *Vita S. Winwaloei* in both consists, first, of a metrical preface: *Incipit praefatio vitae sancti Winwaloei Cornugillensis*,[11] in which the author tells us his name:

> "Vita brevi studii contexitur ordine sacri
> Eximii patris monachorum Winwaloei,
> Quam precibus relego fratrum communibus almam
> Vurdestinus et albis conor scribere libris."

Then, after a list of the chapters in both books, and a note as to authors whose books he has made use of, comes Book I in twenty-two chapters, with two passages of moderate length in verse; and Book II in twenty-nine chapters, in which there is a much larger proportion of verse, some whole chapters being entirely metrical. Book III is a metrical recapitulation of the whole *Vita*.

In the British Museum (MS. Cotton. Otho D viii) is a much shorter *Vita S. Wingualoei*. All the verses are omitted, and most (but not all) of the masses of "padding" with which B1 and B2 are crammed have disappeared. Otherwise it is identical with B. Father C. De Smedt, who printed both A & B in *Analecta Bollandiana* in 1888, distinguishing the additional matter contained in B by printing it in smaller type, thought that A might be the primitive Life, to which Wrdisten seems obscurely to refer in a rather cryptic sentence in his little bibliography before Bk I,

[8] The best printed edition is by La Borderie (Rennes, 1888).

[9] B2 omits the *Vita S. Idiuneti*, the charters, and the lists of abbots of Landévennec and counts of Cornouaille.

[10] *Mélanges d'histoire de Cornouaille* (Paris, 1911).

[11] In the Life of S. Guenael, Cornouaille is called *Cornu-Galliae*. Ordericus Vitalis calls Cornwall *Cornu Britanniae*.

"quod sacrae hujus firma hystoriae predicti sancti gestorum radice contraximus." Latouche took the same view, ascribing it to the monk Clement. Wrdisten, he suggested, incorporated it in his own much more voluminous work. Later scholars, such as Duine and Largillière, have abandoned Latouche's suggestion and consider that Wrdisten is the author of A as well as of B, the former being merely a first edition of the latter. The language of A seems to be too similar to the additions in B to make it credible that it could be by a different writer.[12]

We must also consider the possibility of A being, not the original, but an abridgement of B. It is difficult, indeed, when one compares the two versions, placing them side by side, as Latouche has done (*op. cit.*, pp. 11-21), not to accept his conclusion that the long passages found in B and not in A are interpolations, as in several cases these passages end with an apology for digression. Much of the additional matter in B consists, as we have seen, in poems, some of them having little or no connection with the rest of the work. On the other hand, there are several things to be considered which may be regarded as pointing to B as being after all the original. A is an English manuscript, unknown outside England. There are numerous instances of English medieval hagiographers abridging continental Lives which they rightly considered needlessly diffuse (the *Vita Rumonis* is an example). A is (like most English *Vitae*) not divided into chapters, while B is—an abridger naturally discards the division into chapters, especially when he omits many chapters altogether. A, together with two other English Lives of S. Winwaloe which we

[12] Duine, *Mémento des sources hagiographiques de l'histoire de Bretagne* (Rennes, 1918), No. 7. Largillière, *Mélanges d'hagiographie bretonne* (Brest, 1925), p. 15. Since writing the above, I have had the following interesting letter from Mr Neil R. Ker, of the British Museum. It indicates the *provenance* of A, which no one had yet ascertained. He says: "There can be no doubt, I think, that Otho D. viii was written at Canterbury. I judge from the script, which is of the kind written at Canterbury in s. XII—though not of the most marked Canterbury type—and by the relation to the other Canterbury passionals. Also the title *Passionale Sancti Ignatii Primum*, which identifies it with the entry in the medieval catalogue (ed. M. R. James, *Ancient Libraries of Canterbury and Dover*, p. 52, no. 360) is twelfth-century, not much later than the manuscript itself. . . On general grounds I should think it very likely that the Otho copy is an abbreviation of a longer Life." The *Passio S. Ignatii* "is based ultimately," says Mr Robin Flower, "on a Low Country collection." It contains Lives of SS. Vedast, Amand, Ansbert and Austreberta, the last of whom was the patron saint of a very important monastery at Montreuil. The Cardiff Public Library has a manuscript (No. 381) of the middle of the 12th century, which came from the library of Sir George Wombwell, containing Wrdisten's Life, preceded by the Life from manuscripts at Marchiennes and Montreuil printed in the *Acta Sanctorum*, March, vol. i, pp. 252-4 (Paris ed.).

possess,[13] contains, as we shall see, a long episode borrowed from the Life of S. Ethbin, to which there is no reference whatever in B. There are also some details in B not found in A, like the place-name *Breona* in c.15, which seem not to be interpolations, but look like parts of the original omitted by the abridger not specially interested in Brittany. Moreover, it is difficult, if A is the original, to account for the existence of a copy of it in England, while no copy at all exists in France.

We will now analyse the Life of S. Winwaloe, dividing it into chapters, as in B, and noting the principal omissions made by A.

BOOK I

Incipit Vita sancti Wingualoei, quod est V nonas martis.[14]

c.1 begins with a description of "the island of Britain, from which our nation, as common report says, originally came." The inhabitants were punished, as holy Gildas says, for their monstrous crimes by the invasion of the Saxons. A pestilence followed, which a few were able to escape by leaving their native country.

c.2. Among these was a certain illustrious man named Fracanus, a cousin of the British king Catovius—a man most famous in the eyes of the world. The said king ruled over Nomnia [a mistake for *Domnonia*], a country notorious for its sacrileges, unlawful feastings and adulteries.[15] A pestilence was sent to avenge these crimes, and to escape it Fracan crossed the British sea with his two sons, Weithnocus and Jacobus, and their mother Alba, who was called Trimammis, because she had three breasts, according to the number of her sons. She had also a daughter, but it is not the custom to record the names of women when writing genealogies. Fracan landed at the port which is called Brahec, and immediately began a search for a home in the immediate neighbourhood, for it was about the eleventh hour of the day,[15] and found an estate of considerable size, like a parish in extent,[16] surrounded by woods, now bearing the name

[13] *Vita Sancti Winewaloei abbatis* (MS. Bodl. 240, p. 822) is an exact copy of A, except that it omits the Introduction, and starts with the words "Erat in insula Britannica vir quidam illustris," etc. Capgrave's *Nova Legenda Anglie* contains a greatly abbreviated summary of this, made by John of Tynemouth, who has, as usual, omitted most of the proper names and place names and many whole incidents. At the end he adds the statement that the saint was "in suo monasterio Tauraco sepultus," which he must have found in the *Vita Ethbini*, and which of course contradicts Wrdisten's *Vita*. He also gives us a date: "Floruit autem circa annum domini 459." Both these Lives may be found printed in the second volume of Horstman's edition of *Nova Legenda Anglie* (Oxford, 1901). MS. Bodl. 240 came, it is interesting to note, from the abbey of Bury St Edmund. It is thus described in the Summary Catalogue: "Liber monachorum Sancti Edmundi, in quo continetur secunda pars Historie auree, quam scribi fecit dompnus Rogerus de Huntedone sumptibus graciarum suarum anno Domini M. ccc. lxxvij." Its number was H. 55 in the abbey library.

[14] This is the rubric in A.

[15] A omits this clause.

[16] *quasi unius plebis modulum.*

of its discoverer [*i.e.*, Ploufragan], made fertile by a certain river, which is properly called "Blood." He happily entered into possession of it, with his party, and the pestilence did not follow them.

c.3. The colony increases in number and prosperity. Fracan's wife brings forth her third son. He is named Wingualoeus.[17] His mother reared him as a child of noble birth should be reared. As soon as he could speak he learned to praise God. Before long he began to express a desire to be sent to a certain spiritual father that his soul might be cared for and his mind trained in sacred studies, for he longed to join the heavenly choirs who serve God perpetually. But his father did not approve and wished him to remain in the world. One day, however, while the father was with the other shepherds, feeding his flock in the fields, a terrific thunderstorm came on. Fracan was overwhelmed with fear, and at once vowed, not only to put no obstacle in the way of Winwaloe's holy resolve but to devote his other two sons to the Lord as well.

c.4. On his return home Fracan told his wife what had happened, and a week later he took the child to "a certain angelic teacher named Budoc, surnamed The Zealous (*cognomine Arduum*), richly endowed with learning, conspicuous for righteousness, whom all people of that time regarded as a bulwark of the faith and a most firm pillar of the Church." While they were on the way to the island which is called Laurea, where the said light of faith shone [*i.e.*, where this famous master lived], a sudden darkness covered the face of the earth, a storm came down on the sea, and Fracan was terrified. Winwaloe reassures his father in a long and edifying exhortation to trust in the Creator, full of texts from Scripture. The father listened in wonder. Soon after the sun reappeared and the whole of the land which is called Goëllo[18] was bathed in light. The rest of the day was fine.

c.5. As the sun was setting they arrived at their destination. Fracan informed the master of the purpose of his coming. The boy was brought in and, by the inspiration of the Holy Ghost, without anyone telling him to do so, he prostrated himself before the great saint whose disciple he was to be. The master, looking upon him in the spirit of prophecy, foretold to his father his future greatness. Next morning Fracan asked the man of God's blessing and returned to his home in peace. The boy felt no homesickness, as most children do when sent away to school by their parents, but at once began his lessons with the master. He learned the alphabet in one day, made rapid advances in his studies and in course of time acquired a thorough knowledge of the Old and New Testaments.

c.6 contains a little homily on study and self-discipline, entitled *De materia bene conversandi*.[19]

c.7. Soon after, Budoc crossed to the mainland to pray, leaving the boys on the island. One of them broke his leg in a game they were playing. Winwaloe prayed and made the sign of the cross over the fracture, and the child was instantly healed.

c.8. Pious reflections on this miracle, ending with S. Ambrose's hymn *Orabo mente Dominum*.[19]

[17] *puro appellant nomine Wingualoeum.*

[18] "*qui Uelamensis dicitur pagus.*"

[19] A omits.

c.9. Winwaloe's charity to the poor is described, and two lines from "the admirable hymn in his honour, composed by Clement, the servant of Christ, recently snatched away by an untimely death," are quoted:

"cum non haberet terrestres,
gazas praebebat caelestes."

c.10. Pious reflections.[19]

c.11. A jealous scholar hears him addressing spiritual exhortations to the poor and reproves him for not being more practical in his charity. Winwaloe replies gently and proceeds to give sight to a blind man who was standing amid the crowd of mendicants. He wishes the miracle to remain secret, but Budoc, hearing that a blind man had been healed, holds a kind of identification parade of his scholars and the blind man recognizes Winwaloe. Budoc and all his pupils prostrate themselves before him and burst out into a set of elegiac verses in his honour, beginning: "Cantemus sancto, cantemus Guingualoeo"[20]

c.12. Exhortation addressed to Winwaloe by Budoc, bidding him not hide his light under a bushel.[21]

c.13. Pious reflections *de adhaerentibus sanctis*.[22]

c.14. One day, while his only sister Chreirbia, who was still a child, was playing with other girls, a savage gander flew at her, pecked out her eye and swallowed it. The child returned home crying. Great was the grief of her parents. That night an angel appeared to Winwaloe in a dream, informed him what had happened and bade him go to the rescue. Winwaloe set out for his father's house and on his arrival had the flock of geese collected before him. He at once spied the offender, who was much bigger than all the other birds and, following the instructions given him by the angel, ordered him to be cut open. The eye was found and restored to its place, and his sister found that she could see as well as ever. The gander returned to the flock none the worse for the operation, stretching out its long neck in front of it. After comforting his parents, Winwaloe returned to the monastery.

c.15. On another occasion, while one of the disciples committed to his charge, named Tethgonus,[23] was reading over by himself the lesson Winwaloe had just given him, he fell asleep. The warm sun brought a serpent out of its hole, who found the sleeping boy and bit him in the foot. The poison spread all over his body and he was soon at death's door. Winwaloe, to whom he had gone immediately after feeling the bite, pointed out to him the consequences of sloth, and then called forth the reptile from its hole and destroyed it by touching it with the cross he held in his hand. Finally he healed the disciple by making him drink oil mixed with water which he had blessed. Fracan heard of this miracle and asked his son to pray that the place where this happened, which is called Breona,[24] might never again harbour adders. Winwaloe did so, and

19 A omits.

20 These verses, which must obviously have been composed by Wrdisten some time before, are introduced very awkwardly here, especially as in line 11 Winwaloe is hailed as "a disciple of Saint Patrick"! A omits them.

21 Quoted from Clement's hymn, lines 35, 36.

22 A omits.

23 B2 reads *Thetgonus*. A omits the name.

24 A omits this place-name. In B1 a 16-cent. hand has added in the margin "Cap. 4 dicitur *Laurea*."

since then no snakes have ever been seen there and, if any are brought there, they die at once.

c.16. A shepherd called Gouedmon, who was guarding the flocks of his master Quonethed in a wood, was surprised by a thunderstorm one evening. Night came on, and he found himself surrounded by wolves. In an agony of fear he called upon S. Winwaloe to protect him, and a vision of the saint appeared and stood by him all night keeping the wolves back with his staff. In the morning he was able to lead back his flock unharmed. [In B. a hymn of 23 hexameters suitable to the occasion is placed in his mouth]. He visits Winwaloe, who is surprised to hear the shepherd's story, as he is quite unconscious of what has happened.

c.17 (omitted in A) contains references to Old Testament stories recording similar marvels.

c.18. One day a foolish dispute arose between Fracan and Rival, duke of Domnonia, concerning the swiftness of their horses. It was decided to have a race on a given day. A large crowd assembled, the race began, and Fracan's horse was leading, when the boy who rode him, Maglus, son of Conomaglus,[25] Fracan's *nutritor*, was thrown on some sharp rocks and broke all his bones. The accident caused universal consternation and nobody was more grieved than Fracan, who felt that the blame lay on him. Fortunately Winwaloe happened to come up and by his prayers healed the injured lad. This and other miracles caused his fame to spread throughout Armorica.

c.19. One night after Complin, as he lay in bed, a sudden resolve came into his mind to visit the places consecrated by the holy life and labours of S. Patrick who, not long before this time, had, like a candle shining brightly on high, illuminated all the churches of Ireland, and not them only but every part of the world to which his fame had spread. For he had converted, or confounded, all the *magi* and *arioli* in that island, and so had won all men for Christ. Winwaloe determined at once to sail next day to the land of the Scots with some merchants who were in the harbour waiting for a favourable wind.[26] As he thought on these things, a bright light shone in his cell and he saw a man of angelic aspect, richly robed and wearing a crown, who said to him, "Winwaloe, saint of God, dearest brother, think no more of this long journey. I am Patrick, whose land thou desirest to see. All that thou dost wish to learn in a strange land thou canst learn here in thine own country. But thou wilt not remain long in this spot." The apparition then vanished.[27]

c.20–22. Next morning Winwaloe went to the cell in which his master Budoc slept and studied, and, after reverently bowing and asking his blessing and leave to speak, for the rule of silence, except in cases of necessity, was then strictly observed, told him the vision. Budoc was grieved to part with Winwaloe, but told him it was his duty to obey the divine call, and gave him eleven disciples. After a long farewell speech,[28] Budoc embraced each one, beginning with Winwaloe.

[25] A omits these names. Fr De Smedt suggests that *Maglus*, which in Breton means *prince*, may have become a personal name later, in popular tradition.

[26] A omits this and the previous sentence.

[27] In B Patrick's speech is considerably amplified. He says to Winwaloe, "habes et nostri quam vidisti et audisti normam" (? the Celtic monastic rule).

[28] A omits.

BOOK II

c.1 and 2. Next day Winwaloe and his eleven disciples took their leave of Budoc, after receiving his blessing, and set out, not knowing whither to go, but trusting to God to direct them.[29]

c.3 Turning westwards and passing through the regions of Domnonia they reached the borders of Cornouaille (*Cornugillensium confinia*) and at last reached the island which is called Theopepigia [*i.e.*, Tibidy]. It is a cheerless place, exposed to every wind that blows, girt with sharp rocks and unfit for human habitation. Here they set up a little church (*parvo oratorio*) and a few huts, and planted a garden to grow vegetables, and stayed there three years. None of the party died while they were on the island, because it was God's will that they should all be laid to rest near the body of their abbot [at Landévennec]. In the centre of the island there is a hill on which they used to sit and converse. From it they could see in the morning a valley surrounded by wooded hills, from which they were separated by an arm of the sea and the great river called Ampnis [*i.e.*, the Aulne] two miles wide. A mist used to rise at dawn from this valley and the place looked most attractive as the sun rose. They often wished their monastery were there. We have found no mention in the records of our fathers of anything remarkable which happened during their stay on the island.[30]

c.4. Now one day, while they were, as usual, gathered on the aforesaid hill after Terce and were looking across the water at the place where now his sacred body reposes, together with innumerable bodies of other saints, Winwaloe asked the brethren if they were willing to go there. "The very woods you behold," he said, "as the foliage bends towards you [moved by the wind] beseech you to come. Kneel three times and humbly pray that Christ the Lord will show a mighty sign. Then let each of the brethren take the hand of him that is in front of him." They did so, and with his staff he struck the waters, which parted, and they all went through the river on dry land, singing the song which Moses sang after the crossing of the Red Sea.[31]

c.5. They entered the great wood which clothed the shores, and passing through the valley they had so often gazed at from afar, they found a place in shape like a sling [or "drag-net," *fundum in modum fundae formatum*]. It is a peaceful spot, shut in by woods and rocks on one side and by the estuary and river on the other. The entrance is by a steep path (*per declivia montis . . . non facillimus*) from the west, which skirts the enclosure and leads to the gate of the present holy monastery. There is only one gate and it is on the east. The monastery faces east and is surrounded by a wall on either side of the gate, the rest being protected by a ditch, hills clothed with trees, and rocks. The sea washes one flank (*ala*) and the river, winding southward to Mount Araegus, the other. The plot of land thus bounded is protected from every wind, except to a certain extent the east wind, and is warm and in every way delightful. The spring flowers make their earliest appearance there and the autumn leaves linger there longer than anywhere else. It is a kind of Paradise, prepared by God for his servants and, as it is rich in the fruits of the earth, so it is rich in

[29] In B the greater part of c.1 and the whole of c.2 consist of a very long panegyric of Winwaloe, quoting Holy Scripture, "Basil and Penuphius" and other fathers.

[30] A omits this sentence.

[31] B adds a hymn in elegiacs which they sang when they reached the opposite shore.

heavenly fruits. And from the very first down to the present day it has always had this privilege (granted as it were by Winwaloe's own mouth), that no woman has ever entered the place or any of its dependencies.[32]

c.6. The new monastery is compared to a hive of busy bees. The abbot spends all his time in prayer and in meditation on the law of God.

c.7. There was no drinking-water in the monastery and they had to go a long way to get it. One day the disciples, tired of these repeated journeys, asked Winwaloe to give them a water supply. He bade them return to their tasks and, when he was alone, prayed to our Lord Jesus Christ and then traced a circle on the ground with the end of his staff. Straightway a copious fountain appeared, and a stream from it began to run eastwards towards the shore. When the brethren came back from their work, they rejoiced at this great miracle and glorified the Lord in his saint, who had already showed himself a second Moses and had now proved to be another Aaron.

c.8. One night, while he was praying alone in the oratory, a horrible monster appeared to him, of human shape and gigantic size, a phantasy of the Evil One intended to distract his thoughts from God. It mocked the saint and poured forth words of blasphemy. This continued all night. Winwaloe addresses the foul spirit in a long adjuration full of texts from Holy Scripture (omitted in A). Finally the Devil vanishes, leaving behind him a horrible smell. Brother Tethgon, whose cell adjoined the oratory, heard the Devil's reproaches and the saint's replies and, arising, himself beheld the fearsome apparition and afterwards revealed what had happened to the brethren, who were greatly edified.

Chapters 9–11 describe the saint's ascetic practices. From the age of twenty-one till his death he was never seen to sit down in church. He was never dejected, never unduly elated, he never laughed at anyone, he was always modest and humble, calm and courteous, affable and kind to all, never angry, and in aspect like an angel.[33] As a child he had always rendered entire obedience to Saint Budoc, from whose word and example he had learned true religion, so that when he was a man none among the clergy showed such grace as he. He was accustomed daily to repeat the entire psalter, with his arms outstretched in the form of a cross, standing motionless or kneeling. From the time he built the monastery he never wore woollen or linen, but clothes made of goats' hair. He slept in the clothes he wore during the day, on a hard bed, in which were no bedclothes nor even straw but only birch-bark fibre, with a stone for pillow. He never tasted wheaten bread except in the Eucharist, otherwise he ate barley bread, which he mingled with ashes (in remembrance of Ps. 102:9), and a relish of flour and herbs. In Lent he used to abstain each week from all

[32] The description of Landévennec in c.6 and 7 is omitted in A. In the cartulary a specific reason is given for the entrance of the monastery being prohibited to all women. "A certain man named Petranus came one night secretly to the House of S. Guengualoeus, while his wife slept, to hear the words of the said saint. When his wife awoke, she went, at the instigation of the Devil, to seek for her husband and beat him in the choir. No woman has since entered that choir" (No. LXVIII).

[33] By the kind help of Dom Paul Ringeval, monk of Solesmes, I have been able to identify a sentence in the passage I have here paraphrased as a word-for-word quotation from the *Vita S. Germani, abbatis Grandivallensis* (Grandvilliers, or Munsterthal), who died *c.* 661, by the monk Bobolenus: "Erat enim adspectu angelicus, sermone nitidus, opere sanctus, corpore integer, ingenio optimus, consilio magnus, fide catholicus, spe patientissimus, caritate diffusus." The same passage is also quoted in the *Vita Mereadoci*.

food on certain days. On Saturday and Sunday he ate a little cheese. On Sunday also he took a few small fishes, in honour of the holy Resurrection. But he never touched the flesh of any animal or bird, or any kind of animal fat except what was made of milk, and that only on the days aforesaid. His drink was water, or cider made of wild apples. Wine (except for the Eucharist) was unknown in the monastery of Winwaloe.

Such was the rule observed in this monastery for many years, that is, from the time when Gradlon, called "the Great", ruled Brittany, down to the fifth year of the reign of the most pious Emperor Louis, in the year of our Lord's incarnation 818. By this time the rule had begun to be felt to be too severe. In addition to the privations already described, each monk had only a tunic to wear by night or day, with a sheepskin and footgear, and a little mantle (*palliolum*) when he was obliged to travel. Whence it came to pass that the most serene emperor aforesaid, when he had fixed his camp in this province of Brittany, on the river Ellé (*Elegius*), near the forest which is called Priziac (*Brisiaci*), sent to the monastery this mandate, written by his own hand, as follows.

c.13. (Edict of Louis the Pious: omitted in A).

"In the name of our Lord God and Saviour Jesus Christ, Louis, by the operation of Divine Providence Emperor, Augustus, to all the bishops and to the whole ecclesiastical order in Brittany. Be it known to you that when Matmonoc, abbot of the Monastery of Landevinnoch, appeared before us, and we had questioned him both concerning the manner of life of the monks who dwell in the monasteries of those parts and concerning their tonsure, and had been fully informed as to these matters, and ascertained that they were traditions received from the Scots [*i.e.* the Irish], and since the order of all the holy, apostolic and Roman church is very different, we thought it good that those committed to our charge, by the dispensation of God, should agree with the customs of the Universal Church, both in their rule of life and their tonsure; we have therefore ordered that they should live according to the rule of the holy father Benedict, which is both practicable (*possibilis*) and worthy of praise, and that as regards the tonsure they should fall into line with the practice of the holy Roman church, which is spread throughout the world, and that in this monastery aforesaid, and in others subject to it which may be able fully to obey our command, they should observe the same manner of life according to that which in the rule of the holy and glorious father Benedict is written. These precepts of the most pious Emperor Louis are confirmed by his own hand.

The seal of the most serene	*Monogramma*	Louis Emperor."

The observance of this rule of Father Benedict was begun in the same year in the aforesaid monastery.

c.14. When the saint was reciting the psalter alone, while the other monks were engaged in their allotted tasks, he used to finish by making a hundred genuflexions. He did this every day, and again at night.[34]

[34] A omits.

Chapters 15–21 consist of a set of poems of unequal length, written in hexameters. None of them appear in A. In the first three we are told that the saint's fame reaches King Gradlon, who is vaguely described as "Cornubiensium rex" and "occiduae partis moderator Cornubiorum," who has defeated the Normans in five battles on the river Loire. He goes to see Winwaloe, who addresses him in a long oration, bidding him despise the world and its riches. Gradlon promises to observe all his counsels. He became gentle and merciful, and at last exchanged an earthly kingdom for a heavenly one.

In c.18 Gradlon offers Winwaloe many valuable gifts. Winwaloe refuses them, but at last accepts one, at the prayer of Riocus, a holy man of great virtue, presbyter and monk.[35]

In c.19, entitled *De altitudine et nobilitate Cornubie*, Wrdisten describes Gradlon, *Courentinus* and Winwaloe as the three great luminaries and pillars of Cornouaille, but they had been preceded by the famous *Tutualus*, who was an example to all monks.[36] Wrdisten records a miracle attributed to Tudual: he carried fire in his lap without his clothes being burnt.

Chapters 20 and 21 lament the "subjection" of Cornouaille, and prophesy its future restoration, but in such vague terms that it is impossible to understand what it is to which the poet refers.

c.22. A certain disciple[37] heard that his mother was ill and asked leave to visit her. Winwaloe was reluctant to allow this, but finally the disciple extracted the desired permission. The saint, who foresaw that he would find her dead when he reached home, gave him some holy water, and when he (Rioc) arrived and found that she was indeed dead, he sprinkled the corpse with it and the dead woman returned to life. On being questioned as to her experiences in the unseen world, she related that her spirit had been delivered from the attacks of demons by the intervention of Saint Winwaloe. She spent the rest of her life in good works.

A here inserts the following story:

It was the custom of the blessed Winwaloe to go frequently to a church a mile away to celebrate Mass, accompanied by a distinguished young man, "a great deacon," named Ethbin. It came to pass one day that, as they were passing through the fields in time of harvest, they perceived by the wayside a leper suffering terribly from sores all over his body. His nose was one huge ulcer. Winwaloe put the book he was carrying on the ground, stooped and placed his lips to the sore to suck out the venom, but instead he found himself feeding on the flesh of the Son of God.[38] Ethbin, who was helping to support the

[35] These verses are somwhat ambiguous. Charter XXI in the cartulary, entitled *De Lan Rioc*, relates that "Saint Rioc, whose mother was raised from the dead by the power of S. Winwaloe, made a special offering to God and to S. Winwaloe of all her heritage *sibi separatam ab omnibus parentibus . . . in monachiam perpetuam*. Gradlon confirms the gift. The cartulary (No. XI) shows that there was a place (unidentified) near Crozon called *Sent Rioc*.

[36] Jamque tamen ternos praecesserat ordine sanctus
Eximius isto Tutualus nomine clarus,
Cum meritis monachus multorum exemplar habendus, etc.

[37] B. gives his name, *Rihocus*.

[38] The following detail, seemingly rather inconsistent, is added: "petra mirabilis in ore ejus cecidit."

sick man, looked up and saw over the leper's head the holy cross and angels descending from Heaven, and a voice said, "My servants, ye have not been ashamed of me in my tribulation and I will not be ashamed of you in the kingdom of my Father. Your inheritance is with me, and all who remember you in their prayers shall find salvation in my kingdom." The vision then disappeared. Each of the two saints ascribed the marvel to the merits of the other, and on returning to the monastery both held their peace as to what had happened.

c.23 and 24. There was a certain man at this time called Catamaglus, whose three sons were robbers. Hearing that great treasures from all the country round were stored at the abbey, they resolved to plunder it, and one night, when it was dark, they came by water, made fast their boat to the shore and entered the monastic precincts. In the centre they found a large barn, and were surprised to see it open and brilliantly illuminated. It contained no treasure, however, but only a large store of barley, with which they proceeded to fill their sacks. Meanwhile the monks were singing Matins in church. Winwaloe was perfectly aware of what was happening, and at the conclusion of the office broke the rule of silence (observed in every monastic community at night) to inform the brethren, but bade them do nothing and leave the matter in God's hands. The rule of silence was then re-imposed. The robbers, having filled their sacks, determined to return to their boat, but one fell and broke his leg, the second became rooted to the ground like a tree, and the third was struck blind. The man they had left behind in charge of the boat began to shout and curse his confederates for not coming back to give him his share of the spoil. In the morning, after Prime, Winwaloe told the monks what had happened. They went to the barn, and the saint midly reproached the robbers for what they had done, telling them that they had only to ask at the monastery for what they needed and it would be given them freely. He then healed them. The robbers were converted and entered the abbey as monks.

c.25 contains a little homily on the above story (the words "ecce, fratres carissimi" suggest that it had been read to the monks by Wrdisten.) A omits it, together with two long exhortations which B places in the mouth of Winwaloe in c.24.

c.26. In the first monastery (*eodem loco*) no one could die, though the infirmities of old age could not be excluded. The oldest of the monks, burdened by the weight of many years, longed to be dissolved and released from "this cumbering frame of clay,"[39] and to receive the reward of their labours. At last the reason why death would not come was discovered. We have often (Wrdisten says) heard men of great sanctity say that they had known those of the past generation who had seen a space in heaven open over the monastery of exactly the same size as that which it occupied on earth, and angels ascending and descending upon it, as in Jacob's dream. And this was the reason that they could not die where life eternal was seen. Consequently the monks compelled Winwaloe to pull down the abbey and rebuild it towards the east, by the shore. The new monastery, in which Winwaloe's bones and those of his companions now rest, is only a stone's throw away from the site of the original one, and within the same enclosure. The gentle murmur of the little stream flowing by it seems to speak to those who live there of rest after toil. It has been favoured

[39] "gravi isto corpore," a quotation from the Complin hymn "Christe, qui lux es et dies."

with the same angelic visions as the older house, and soon after it had been built an angel appeared to Winwaloe as he was praying in the oratory alone after Complin and told him that the ripe corn would now be gathered. Shortly afterwards the oldest monk died, and others followed, but still in order of age, for none as yet could die except of old age and the oldest always died first. And this was long the rule in the monastery and has only recently been changed. (B adds a fragment of a homily on preparation for death, ending with a doxology.)

c.27. At this very time a certain noble lady suddenly became blind. She bore the affliction with exemplary patience and continued steadfastly in prayer and thanksgiving. One night she saw in a dream an angel who bade her go to Winwaloe. Next morning she was led to his presence by her son and told him the words of the angel. He touched her eyes with his right hand, and she received her sight and returned, glorifying God.

c.28. At last an angel announced to Winwaloe that the hour of his departure had come, and that those who had gone before him to the heavenly city were waiting for him. For it has been handed down by aged and holy men that many of that congregation had predeceased him and had been buried by his own hand in one cemetery, which is called *Reliquiae sanctorum*.[40] Winwaloe called the brethren and informed them of what had been told him. He bade them elect as his successor "a pastor who should be sweet as honey and bitter as absinth. Seek not for peace with the world here, in order that ye may enjoy tranquillity and peace in Heaven, where is supreme peace and supreme tranquillity." Winwaloe continued to exhort them until the bell rang for Terce. Then, putting on the sacred vestments, he offered Mass and, having received the sacred mystery of the Lord's body and blood, he stood before the altar, supported by a monk on each side, and, joining with his brethren who were singing the praises of God and with the angelic choirs who are present at our worship, he yielded up his pure spirit to Jesus Christ. It was the third of March, the Wednesday after Ash Wednesday. The brethren buried his most holy body with due honour, amid psalms and hymns and spiritual songs, giving thanks to God and to our Lord Jesus Christ, who with the Father and the Holy Ghost liveth and reigneth for ever and ever. Amen.

Explicit Vita sancti Wingualoei confessoris.

At the end of the homily composed for annual reading at the saint's festival, in which Wrdisten has summed up his Life of S. Winwaloe, he adds this interesting statement: "His body was translated from the little church into the great church where we keep it to-day, and we celebrate this translation on April 28. Our fathers have established this custom, to avoid the inconvenience of his festival falling in Lent." "This passage," as Duine remarks, "shows that some critics [*e.g.* Latouche] have gone too far in questioning whether Winwaloe ever came to Brittany or founded Landévennec. We have here a trustworthy liturgical

[40] A omits.

tradition."[41] The date of his death on March 3 was honoured liturgically in an older church. A larger church was afterwards built and the saint's body was translated into it, apparently at some period before the ninth century, so that Wrdisten could say that "antiquiores patres" had instituted a festival to commemorate this translation, which had already become the chief feast of the saint. In this connection it is interesting to note that the parallel passage in the second Life of Winwaloe printed in the Bollandist *Acta Sanctorum* (a homily contained in manuscripts belonging to the abbeys of Montreuil and Marchiennes) states that the older church was of wood: "sepultusque est in ecclesia lignea, quam ipse laudabili opere jusserat fabricari."[42] This may well be a tradition brought by the monks of Landévennec to Montreuil in 914.

§

The Life we have analysed for the English reader is full of interest. In spite of all its obvious faults—its pages of useless padding, the legendary character of many of the incidents, and the crabbed Latin of Wrdisten's hexameters, of which it is often difficult to see the exact meaning, we must be thankful that he wrote it, for otherwise we should know nothing more about Winwaloe than we know of so many other Cornish and Breton saints, of whom we have only the bare names (*nuda nomina*, as William of Malmesbury says). It is something to possess the unbroken tradition of a great Breton monastery about its foundation, written before the destruction of records caused by the occupation of Brittany by the Norsemen in the tenth century. Of no other British religious house in Celtic times have we such a detailed description as we possess, thanks to Wrdisten, of Landévennec. A contrast with the *Vita Corentini* will show us what we should have lost if he had not written. The Life of S. Corentin is nothing more than a collection of late folklore. The traditions of Quimper had been forgotten when its clergy desired to have in writing the story of its saintly founder, while for S. Winwaloe

[41] *Mémento* . . . No. 7, pp. 40–1.

[42] This *Vita* contains several statements about Winwaloe's death not found in A or B. The saint gives communion to all the brethren before breathing his last. With uplifted hands he makes a short prayer, commending them to the Lord—"Domine Jesu Christe, pastor bone, commendo tibi oves," etc. At the moment of his death the right hand of the Lord is seen to descend through the roof of the church to receive his spirit.

we have a fairly complete record of the stories told about the founder of Landévennec not more than about 250 years after his death, made in the place where he had lived and where his tomb was honoured and annual festivals and visible memorials, and perhaps written as well as oral traditions, preserved the memory of at any rate some incidents in his life.

We must not indeed expect to find in Wrdisten's book a real biography of S. Winwaloe. A good biography needs contemporary evidence and a skilled writer to select and record it. Without these the most remarkable characters become in a century or so dim, far-off figures and their doings are entirely forgotten. Now more than two centuries had passed when our author wrote.

Wrdisten is a poet and litterateur. He shares to the full in the tendency of poets and litterateurs to try to improve on the truth by adding to it picturesque fancies. For years he had been writing poems in honour of the patron saint of his monastery, not entirely forgetting others connected with his native Cornouaille, and collecting traditions about Winwaloe and Landévennec. His work is of very unequal merit. It contains touches of real poetic feeling, such as the vision of the sun illuminating the shores of Goëllo as Fracan and Winwaloe make their way to Laurea, and the delightful pen-pictures of Landévennec and its monastery—its babbling stream, its balmy climate, its wooded heights. Other sections of his work are much less happy. In c.11 of Book I we have a good example of how he has worked up a slight tradition (if indeed it is not a pure invention of his own) with great pains, but not with sufficient skill to make the story in the least convincing, and then placed in the mouths of the master and scholars of Laurea a poem he had written some time before, which not only does not suit the story but actually contradicts it. We may probably assume with safety that the historical value of most of the incidents in Book I is very slight indeed. It is in Book II, when Winwaloe settles at Landévennec, that we come to more trustworthy traditions.

What materials had Wrdisten to work on when he started to prepare a Life of S. Winwaloe?

At the beginning of Book I he gives us a list of his sources, nearly all of which (Augustine, Cassiodorus, etc.) are of course only the sources of the pious reflections with which he has so liberally garnished his pages. But among them he includes a "history of the doings of the saint." In the preface to Book II he says he used "ancient writings" as well as "majorum relatio venerabilium" for the first book and for the second he has also information "sive ex scriptis, sive relatu." These vague words in all probability mean a written *Vita*. Latouche thought that the text he calls A was this older Life, and that it had been written by the monk Clement to whom Wrdisten refers. His suggestion has been generally abandoned nowadays, as I have said, but Wrdisten is no doubt to be trusted when he says that the hymn "Alme dignanter supplicum" was the work of Clement. This lengthy composition, which contains two lines borrowed from the well-known "Martyr Dei qui unicum,"[43] is a kind of versified panegyric of the saint. In several of the verses there are references to anecdotes which Wrdisten has introduced into his work, though not in the same order, and Wrdisten quotes two lines from it *verbatim*. Clement calls Winwaloe in verse 2 "Britigena." He devotes four verses to the school where Winwaloe was educated, though he does not mention Budoc. He relates the stories of the fellow pupil who broke his leg and of the disciple bitten by a snake, and the miracles of the passing through the sea to Landévennec and of the fountain the saint caused to spring up there. One verse deals with the story of the three robbers, and another refers to the influence the saint exercised over "Gradlonum, ducem patriae," which is followed by an account of his sister (her name is not mentioned) having her eye pecked out by the gander. There are two miracles mentioned in Clement's poem which Wrdisten has not inserted in his work. One of them, describing a chieftain's son being cured of violent toothache, is explained by Charter XXX in the cartulary.[44]

Now it is clear that we have here the outline of a considerable part of the subject-matter of Wrdisten's Life of S. Winwaloe. Clement's verses of course merely refer briefly to well-known anecdotes more fully described in a narrative familar to everyone at Landévennec. They postulate the existence of a fairly long Life of the saint, already committed to writing by the middle of the ninth century, and perhaps considerably earlier. I think that we may be quite sure that Wrdisten had before him such a Life,

[43] Part of the Benedictine rite recently introduced at Landévennec.

[44] This charter tells us that the island of Terenes is properly *Dant Enes*, and was given to S. Winwaloe by Maeluc Dant Hir (="Long Tooth") for healing his son Pritient Liusuc of toothache.

which we may call the "Original Life," as well as Clement's hymn, when he began his great literary effort.

The second verse of Clement's hymn describes Winwaloe as "Britigena." The Original Life must have begun with some of the statements contained in cc.1 and 2 of Wrdisten's elaborate composition. The latter explains *Britigena* by reminding his readers that the colonization of Armorica by immigrants from Great Britain is a national tradition. Unfortunately he gives us no details whatever as to exactly what the Breton tradition on this all-important subject in the ninth century was, but proceeds to quote "Saint Gildas," so we are no wiser than we were before.

In c.2 Wrdisten begins the story of Winwaloe. We are told the names of his father and mother and his two brothers, and how the family came from Great Britain and settled in Armorican Domnonia, where Winwaloe is born. The remaining chapters of Book I describe his education in the school of Budoc.

Now the chief thing for us to notice in the first book of Wrdisten's *Vita Winwaloei* is the fact that there was a very definite tradition at Landévennec, already embodied in a written Life, connecting the saint with the neighbourhood of Saint-Brieuc. Many of the stories contained in these early chapters are found in, and perhaps copied from, other Lives of Celtic saints. The anecdote of the boy thrown from his horse in a race is found in the *Vita Samsonis* and so is the story of the saint healing a companion bitten by a snake. The master's prophecy of the future greatness of his pupil reminds us of Eltut's similar prophecy in the *Vita Samsonis*, c.9. Rigual and "the river which is called Blood" both appear in the *Vita Brioci*, which also contains a story about wolves and another about a demoniacal apparition very like that in Book II, c.8. But the mention of the immunity of "the place which is called Breona"[45] from the presence of adders is obviously a local tradition, and it is clear that the author of the Original Life knew Ploufragan, the river Gouet which flows through it, the Pays de Goëllo, Brehec (halfway between Saint-Brieuc and Laurea) and the Paimpol archipelago very well indeed[46] and had reason for associating his hero with this district.

Wrdisten identifies Winwaloe's father with the eponym of the great parish of Ploufragan, which adjoins the city of Saint-Brieuc

[45] *Breona* has not been identified.

[46] We can hardly think that Wrdisten knew Saint-Brieuc or he would surely not have made Fracan arrive at Brehec at 5 p.m. and settle down at Ploufragan the same evening.

on the south. It seems impossible that he should have made Fracan the father of Winwaloe unless there was already some tradition connecting the latter with Ploufragan. Since the appearance of *Les Saints et l'organisation chrétienne primitive dans l'Armorique* in 1925, the older theory (put forward by La Borderie), that the numerous parishes in Brittany beginning with *Plou* (=*Plebs*) got their names from the chieftains of clans who had colonized the districts in question, has been generally abandoned in favour of Largillière's contention that the parish is called after its spiritual, not its temporal, founder. Wrdisten's story seems to conflict with the latter view. It does not however necessarily disprove it. We cannot be sure that Fracan was in reality exactly what Wrdisten represents him to have been. There is a Breton saint of almost identical name (*Frogan*) invoked in the Litany of Limoges. The late Joseph Loth identified Fracan with the eponym of Saint-Frégan (wrongly spelt Frégant), a *trève* of Guisseny in Léon. It may be worth noting that an inscribed stone at Cardinham in Cornwall contains the name *Vrochanus*. Charter XXIII in the Cartulary of Landévennec shows that among the most ancient possessions of the abbey was a place called *Tirifrechan*, the site of which is unknown.

Wrdisten tells us that Fracan was a cousin of "the most famous British king Catovius." This is a very early reference to an important figure in Welsh folk-lore. The twelfth century *Vita Carantoci* tells us that when Carantoc landed at Carrum in Somerset "Cato and Arthur ruled in that country" (John of Tynemouth, in his copy of this *Vita*, reads *Catho*). It looks as if originally, before the time of Geoffrey of Monmouth, King Catov's place in British tradition equalled that of Arthur.[47]

Winwaloe himself bears a genuine British name. We find a *Guingual* in the Book of Llandaff (ed. 1893, p. 169), and M. Vendryes says that it is derived from an older *Vindo-valo*.

[47] *Cathov, filius Gerentonis*, appears in the "Genealogy of Saint Winnoc," and as "Cado, son of Geraint," we find him in the early fifteenth-century pedigrees in the manuscripts of Jesus College, Oxford. The *Myvyrian Archaiology* also speaks of "Cataw, son of Geraint ap Erbyn." The "Epitome of the History of Britain" (Rees's *Lives of the Cambro-British Saints*, p. 616) mentions a "Constantine son of Cador Duke of Cornwall," whom Geoffrey of Monmouth introduces into his romance. In the Tale of Culhwch and Olwen in the *Mabinogion* Caw is in one passage called *Cado*. *Cadwy* appears in the Triads. Catonus, son of Gerentonus, and father of Urbienus, father of Gwitholus, father of Deroch, who was father of Urbienus and Rivalus Murmathon, is a Breton genealogy, given by Morice, *Preuves*, vol. 1, col. 14-15 (It comes from the Chronicle of St-Brieuc, and is apparently taken originally from Ingomar, a Saint-Méen writer of the 11th century.) La Touche has very rashly suggested that "it may be permissible to equate Catovius with S. Cadoc."

The name of Winwaloe's mother introduces an interesting problem. Wrdisten's mention of "genealogies" shows us that he got her name form a Welsh genealogy. We find in fact the entry "Kadvan Sant yn Enlli ap Aeenas Ledewic o Lydaw, a Gwen Teirbron verch Emyr Llydaw i vam" as No. 18 in *Bonedd y Saint* (="The Descent of the Saints")[48]. Cadfan, Gwen Teirbron's son, we may observe by the way, is honoured in Cornouaille, in a chapel on the eastern slope of Mont-Saint-Michel, not far from Landévennec.[49] The name of Winwaloe's sister Chreirbia also appears in *Bonedd y Saint* (No. 14: "a Chreirwy verch Glydno Eidin i vam"). Wrdisten's statements are the earliest evidence we possess for the existence of these genealogies. It seems difficult however to believe that he had seen *Bonedd y Saint* as we know it to-day, for he denies that genealogies reckon the names of women and, as we have just seen, the names of both Gwen and Chreirwy are found in *Bonedd y Saint*. Moreover *Bonedd y Saint* does not give Winwaloe, Weithnoc, Jacobus or Chreirwy among Gwen's children. I think we may conclude that the legend that Winwaloe, Weithnoc and Jacobus were three brothers was well established when Wrdisten wrote, and that it suggested to him the idea of making Alba Trimammis (Guen Teirbron) their mother, since, he thought, he could thus explain a name which puzzled him (and, doubtless, others). It is curious that Wrdisten says nothing more about Weithnoc or Jacobus. One would have thought that the name of Landévennec would have tempted him.

The cult of S. Weithnoc will be dealt with later on. *Jacobus* is the *Saint Jacut* who has a considerable cult in the east of Brittany. He was patron of the important abbey of Saint-Jacut on the north coast (not far from Saint-Malo), which formed an *enclave* of the diocese of Dol. The chief festival observed in the abbey was that of the two saints *Jacutus et Guethenocus*, honoured on the same day (July 5) as a feast of *triplex* rank S. Jacut was also honoured there separately on Feb. 8, and S. Guethenoc on November 5. (The fifteenth-century Missal of Saint-Malo also honoured the

[48] A. W. Wade-Evans has printed one of the manuscripts of *Bonedd y Saint* in *Archaeologia Cambrensis*, 1931, pp. 158f. The oldest manuscript is early thirteenth-century.

[49] Ste Guen had a chapel (now destroyed) in Ploufragan. She is eponym of Ste-Guen (C.-du-N.), and has a statue in the chapel of Rosquelfen in Laniscat. She has a statue in the chapel of Saint-Vennec near Quimper, where she is represented with three breasts, with S. Winwaloe on her lap, and his brothers at her side; also in a seventeenth-century painting of the profession of S. Guénolé in the chapel (dedicated to St. Guénolé) of the *manoir* of Lesven in the parish of Plouguin near Ploudalmézeau (on the coast north of Brest, not far, it may be noted, from Saint-Frégant).

Translacio sci Iacuti et Guehenoci conf. on July 5 and S. Jacut on February 8). A *Vita Jacuti* exists in a manuscript of the thirteenth century. Duine describes it as "a detached branch of the *Vita Winwaloei*, adorned with popular traditions and monastic traditions."[50] Its author tells us that numerous places in Brittany bear the names of Jacut or Guethenoc. The former is still the patron of Saint-Jacut-du-Mené, and of a chapel in Plestin in the Côtes-du-Nord. He also has a statue at Langueux. In the Vannetais he is patron of a parish in the valley of the Oust near Redon—a district full of dedications to saints of Glamorgan, including S. Petroc (it is worth noting that S. Petroc is patron of Trégon, close to the abbey of Saint-Jacut, and that his name is in the kalendar of the abbey).

Chreirbia, on the other hand, is, apart from the *Vita Winwaloei*, unknown in Brittany. The story of Winwaloe's healing her eye, pecked out by a gander, is certainly not "common form." La Touche quotes Mme Fawtier as having suggested that it was a piece of Welsh folk-lore, but unfortunately he has given no reference as to where such a story might be found. *Chreirbia* is certainly a Welsh name, as we have seen. Owen Pughe's Welsh Dictionary gives the word *creirwy*[51] as meaning "a jewel: an epithet for a fine woman, and a proper name," Latouche thinks that Wrdisten was aware of the signification of the name, and consequently describes Winwaloe's sister as *puella pulcherrima*.

The description of Budoc in c.5 is of the very greatest interest. It is certainly based on an ancient tradition. The connection of S. Winwaloe with S. Budoc is confirmed by a very considerable amount of independent evidence. I return to this important question later on.

No scholar has yet attempted to throw any light on the identity of *Tethgon* (or *Thetgon*) who appears twice in the *Vita*. Wrdisten must have had some reason for inserting his name, but it seems impossible to guess what it was. Tethgon does not seem to be honoured as a saint anywhere in Brittany, but the name is no doubt a genuine one. There was a saint of Redon of similar

[50] *Mémento*, No. 75, *Origines Bretonnes*, pp. 12, 13. The *Vita SS. Guethenoci et Iacuti* has been printed by the Bollandists in *Acta Sanctorum*, November, vol. iii. The origin of the abbey is unknown. It does not appear in history before the eleventh century. In the twelfth century it was well endowed, and owned churches even in England.

[51] Quoted by Latouche, *op. cit.* p. 32, no. 2. The latter has by mistake printed *Cheirwy* for *creirwy*. Mr R. Morton Nance remarks that the *ch* in the Breton forms is not the guttural *c'h*, but an old way of spelling *K*.

name mentioned in the Redon Cartulary, *Reliquiae Sti Thetvii:* M. Loth says the correct form of his name is certainly *Tethwiw* (*Noms*, p. 119).

I do not suppose it is possible to explain the reason for the insertion of the vision of S. Patrick in c.19, unless we suppose that it may perhaps have been considered in Wrdisten's time not desirable to encourage visits to Irish monastic schools. His description of Patrick's labours in Ireland shows acquaintance with Muirchu Maccu-Machtheni's Life of the saint. We observe also that he ascribes to Winwaloe S. Patrick's custom of genuflecting 100 times every day and again 100 times at night.[52] There was evidently some kind of tradition at Landévennec that Winwaloe had been a disciple of Patrick, to which Wrdisten refers, but without approving it, as of course it conflicted with his Life of the saint, and was obviously historically impossible. S. Patrick was honoured at Landévennec. His name, written in large letters, appears in the eleventh-century kalendar of the abbey. It is to be observed that the popularity of the cult of S. Patrick is very noticeable in the parts of Normandy evangelized by S. Samson and the Celtic monks of Dol and Alet. There are, *e.g.*, four dedications to him in the Côtentin—at Saint-Patrice-de-Claids, Fierville, Hyenville and Huberville, near the church of S. Méen at Ste-Mère-Église and that of S. *Guingalais* at Auville. Probably devotion to S. Patrick was inculcated in all the enclaves of Dol. Wrdisten's mention of "merchants carrying overseas goods, waiting in the port for a fair wind . . . to cross to the Scots" is an interesting proof of regular trade relations between Ireland and Brittany in the ninth century. A capital found in the ruins of Landévennec Abbey has been thought to show Irish designs. Irish influence, says Dom L. Gougaud, appears to have been felt at Landévennec more than in any other Breton monastery.[53] Latouche (*op. cit.*, p. 80) attempts to use this guarded suggestion as a proof for his absolutely unjustifiable supposition, put forward as if it were an ascertained fact, that "the only fact of which we can be sure in the early history of Cornouaille is the foundation by Irish monks of a monastery in the peninsula of Crozon." Thus a new false "tradition" has been created, as if we had not enough already. Dom Gougaud definitely repudiates it. Very

[52] The author of the Anglo-Saxon Homily on S. Neot has imitated Wrdisten by appropriating the practice for his hero, and the author of the *Vita Mereadoci* has done the same, while increasing the number from 100 to 1000.

[53] *Les Chrétientés celtiques*, p. 123, *Christianity in Celtic Lands*, p. 117.

few, if any, of our Cornish and Breton churches seem to have been founded by Irish missionaries. Louis the Pious was misinformed when he attributed the Celtic tonsure in use at Landévennec to the influence of "the Scots" (cf. *Christianity in Celtic Lands*, pp. 203–4).

In Book II the local traditions of Landévennec appear. There was evidently a very ancient tradition in the abbey, which we may reasonably accept as true, that the monastery had orginally been on the island of Tibidy. The Celtic monks liked to settle on islands. S. Paul Aurelian and S. Magloire both did so. The easternmost of the Isles of Scilly were once inhabited entirely by monks and hermits. This little study will show, I hope, the important part played in Breton ecclesiastical history by the island monasteries near Paimpol. Other well known island monasteries on the inland sea of Etel are described in the Lives of S. Gudwal and S. Cadoe. The cartulary shows that the famous Île de Sein, once (it is said) inhabited by nine Druid sorceresses, belonged to the monastery of Landévennec. Albert Le Grand, following no doubt a tradition current in the seventeenth century, tells us that Winwaloe began his heremitical career by a stay on that island. Tibidy (the word means "House of prayer"[54]) remained for centuries a holy place, and charter LV in the cartulary tells us that "the feast of the church of S. Guy(n)galoeus in the island which is called *Thopepigia* is on the first Sunday in June every year, on which day great indulgences are granted to those who visit the aforesaid church." Near the island, on the mainland, were two places called Lan Meren and Silin, belonging to the monastery from the earliest times, and a vineyard the boundary of which was marked by "the stone which is called *Padrun sancti Uuingualoei*, on which is carved the sign of the holy cross."[55]

We are not surprised to read in c.7 that the well at Landévennec

[54] No explanation has ever been offered of the name of Tibidy in the *Vita* and the Cartulary, *Theopepigia*, or *Thopopegia*. Loth passes it over without comment in his *Chrestomathie bretonne* (presumably as hopeless). Mr R. Morton Nance says, "I wonder if it can have been Greek originally." It is very tempting to suggest that some abbot who knew Greek gave this specially venerated sanctuary a Greek name suggested by Heb. 8: 2 (*cf.* Num. 24: 6, LXX.), especially as the famous church of Towyn was reputed to have been founded by S. Cadfan "after a divine model." This would make excellent sense, but the name would not be in accordance with the strict rules of Greek grammar. (Greek was known in Celtic monasteries, and words from the Greek Testament were used in Lives of Celtic saints).

[55] This is one of the earliest documentary references to stones with crosses cut on them in Brittany. M. Marsille has shown (*Bull. de la Soc. Polymathique du Morbihan*, 1937, pp. 18f.) that there were no crosses in Brittany, other than Greek crosses cut on the face of christianized menhirs, before the twelfth century. Loth explained *Padrun* as being derived from Lat. *perronem*, Fr. *perron*; it means "a kind of chair on which suzerains sat to receive their vassals" in the *Chanson de Roland*.

was believed to have been caused to spring up by the prayers of S. Winwaloe. There are few Lives of Celtic saints which do not contain a similar story. Albert Le Grand tells us that the spring still supplied the monastery with water in the seventeenth century and that it was called *Feunteun Sant Guennolé*. There is also a holy well of St Guénolé at Gouezec, near his chapel.

The traditions about the saint's ascetic habits and the hardness of the rule at Landévennec prior to the introduction of the Rule of S. Benedict in 818 are probably quite true. The statement that Winwaloe did not fast on Saturday is to be noted in proof of the antiquity of these traditions, for at Rome Saturday was a fast. At Milan it was not, as we know from the Life of S. Ambrose, and the Gallican liturgy, from which the Celtic service-books were derived, came from Milan, as Mgr Duchesne has shown.[56] The "diploma" of Louis the Pious is of first-class importance for the early history of Brittany. The reference to the smaller "monasteries subject to Landévennec" is of special interest as showing the monastic organization of the Celtic Breton church. Landévennec seems to have absorbed many older foundations and to have created others—including probably Landewednack in Cornwall.[57]

The poems which form chapters 15-21 contain valuable clues to the early history of Cornouaille. Unfortunately they are largely spoiled by the vagueness of the language, which is only equalled by the poverty of the verses. They tell us that Gradlon, Corentin and Winwaloe were contemporaries, the chief figures in Cornouaille at that time, and that Tutual belonged to the generation before them.[58]

King Gradlon, as Duine remarked, "has had almost as many devoted supporters as the Stuarts."[59] Wrdisten found him in Clement's hymn, and probably in the Original Life, and no doubt there were other traditions about him in the ninth century. We need not deny his existence; Gradlon was a name borne by several Counts of Cornouaille at a later period. But, as the Northmen had not begun their ravages in Europe before the ninth century, Gradlon could not have fought against them if he

[56] Wrdisten quotes the hymns of S. Ambrose, and introduces the one beginning "Orabo mente Dominum" with the words "sancti Ambrosii secundum apostolum [1 Cor. 14: 15] horae sextae roseus hymnus."

[57] The words "quae nostrum plenissime jussum exsequi valuerint" may possibly contain by implication a reference to small monasteries in Cornwall outside the emperor's dominions, where his orders could not be enforced.

[58] Wrdisten does not say that Tutual lived "long" before them, as La Touche asserts.

[59] *Mémento* . . ., No. 231.

lived in the time of S. Winwaloe. What historical foundation there may have been for the victories on the Loire ascribed to him it is impossible to guess.[60] King *Gradalon* appears in c.5 of the *Vita Turiavi* discovered by Duine at Clermont, which seems to have been written at Dol about the very time Wrdisten was writing (it is worth remarking that the latter has, as we have seen, a story about a person raised from the dead being questioned as to what she had seen in the world beyond the tomb which may have been inspired by a similar story in this very same chapter of the *Vita Turiavi*). King Gradlon will also appear in the much later Lives of S. Corentin and S. Ronan. Legends about him continued to grow during the ages. Albert Le Grand in 1636 inserted in his *Vie de S. Guénolé* the well-known fairy-tale about the king and the city of Is.[61] He tells us that in his time the parishes near Landévennec, as Argol, Dinéol, Saint-Nic, Telgruc, Crozon and Châteaulin, used on certain days to go to the abbey and chant a service in the oratory of King Grallon for the repose of his soul. The king's tomb was shown in the abbey, and Le Grand describes it, and quotes the epitaph upon it.

The reference to S. Corentin, by tradition first bishop of Cornouaille, is particularly interesting and is considered in my study of that saint. It will be noticed that Corentin is not introduced by Wrdisten into any story about S. Winwaloe (in fact nothing whatever is told us of the latter's doings outside the monastery after he came to Landévennec).

The mention of Tutual has puzzled many scholars, including La Borderie, as the founder of Tréguier has scarcely any cult in Cornouaille. Largillière has pointed out that there is a parish called Landudal, formerly a *trève* of Briec, and that there is a chapel of Lampabu (Pabu being supposed to be another name for Tudual) in Plouhinec. But both these places are, and must always

[60] It may be that these lines are an interpolation by a writer thinking of Alain Barbetorte's victories.

[61] It may be summarized as follows: King Grallon reigned in the magnificent but wicked and luxurious city of Ys, near Douarnenez. His daughter Dahut was the example and leader of its inhabitants in debauchery. One day Guénolé came to see Grallon. God revealed to him that the hour of punishment had come. "Ah, Sire," he said, "let us leave this place at once, for the wrath of God is about to overwhelm it, your Majesty knows the sins of its people, their measure is full, let us escape before its doom overtakes us." Both leaped on horseback. As they passed through the gates of the city, they turned and saw monstrous waves breaking in and swallowing it up. Dahut had stolen from the king's neck the key which opened the sluices. At that moment Dahut herself appeared and sprang up behind her father. The waves rushed forward in pursuit of the fugitives. Escape seemed impossible. Then a voice was heard saying to the king, "Throw down the devil who is seated behind you." He forced his daughter to leave go, she fell into the waves, which ceased to advance, and the king and Guénolé were saved.

have been, of very little importance, and Wrdisten's words, distinctly stating that he was a pattern for monks, require the existence of some considerable monastery founded by him. Now Loctudy exactly fits the need. In a charter of "Alan Count of Brittany" (No. L in the cartulary), "Guegun, abbatt Tudi," is one of the witnesses, but Charter XXIV, granted by Uurmaelon, Count of Cornwall, and afterwards confirmed at Montreuil, is witnessed by "Huaruuethen, Bishop of Saint Chourentin [*i.e.*, Quimper], Benedict, Abbot of Saint Wingualoaeus, and Uroet, *Abbot of Saint Tutgual*," who is clearly the abbot of Loctudy. We have a further proof of this in the miracle ascribed to Tudual by Wrdisten. No scholar seems yet to have noticed that this is the very miracle ascribed to Bothmael, the companion of Tudy, in the *Vita Maudeti*. There Bothmael carries the live coals across to the island, while Maudez and Tudy watch him. Wrdisten has, whether by accident or design, simply transferred the miracle from one of Maudez's pupils to the other.[62] Wrdisten clearly regarded Tudual and Tudy as being the same.

c.18 and c.22 explain how Landévennec acquired Lanriec, near Concarneau. I have already pointed out how closely the story in c.22 resembles the story in c.5 of the *Vita Turiavi*. At the end of this chapter the manuscript we are calling "A" inserts the episode of the leper. Latouche was wrong in supposing that it formed part of the original Life of S. Winwaloe. If it had, it would have appeared in Wrdisten's complete version (B). What object could there have been in his omitting it? It is only found in English versions of the *Vita*, and may have been interpolated at Canterbury.

Among the relics of the Abbey of Saint-Sauve at Montreuil was the body of a certain *Ethbin*. At some time during the late tenth or eleventh centuries it was desired at Montreuil to have a Life of this saint and a clerk undertook to write one. A good deal of mystery surrounds his work. He seems not to have known Landévennec. He makes Ethbin a Breton, but a disciple of S. Samson, who becomes a monk, not at Landévennec but at "Taurac," where the abbot is called, not Winwaloe but *Similien*. Ethbin has a fellow disciple called Baumerus. The story of the

[62] Charter XLVIII in the cartulary records the grant to the abbey "of a certain *tribus* called *Tref Tudoc* in Plounevez-du-Fou." It has not been identified. The cartulary (No. VII) mentions a place in Telgruc, near Landévennec, called *Lanloebon*, which did *not* belong to the abbey, though the whole of the rest of the parish did. Now *Loevan* is given among the companions of S. Tudual (Loth, *Noms*, p. 81).

leper is related at great length, out of all proportion to the other contents of the Life, and is clearly an interpolation from another book. The saint dies in Ireland. About 1070 Benedict, abbot of Holy Cross at Quimperlé, found in the Ile de Groix part of the head of S. Winwaloe and the relics of certain other saints, among them those of Winwaloe's successor S. Guenaël and of S. Idunet. This latter was patron of Châteaulin and, when the manuscript called B2, which contains the Cartulary of Landévennec, was written, it was desired to have some information about a saint who was regarded, perhaps with reason, as connected with S. Winwaloe. So the author of the cartulary inserted in Charter II a story of how "S. Winwaloe went to visit his brother Ediunetus, who lived on Mount Nin, serving God day and night on the bank of the river which is called Hamm [the Aulne]." The monks of Landévennec wished in addition to have a Life of this saint, so one of them took the *Vita Ethbini* and converted it into a *Vita S. Idiuneti alias dicti Ethbini*. He altered the name into Idiunet in the first two chapters, but left *Ethbin* in the rest. His work was then inserted into B2.

It has been supposed that Ethbin is the eponym of the parish of Pleyben in Cornouaille and that his body was taken to Montreuil at the same time as that of S. Winwaloe. Largillière questions this. It is certain in any case, as we have seen, that the author of the *Vita Ethbini* did not know Landévennec, and in his work Winwaloe is so different from the Winwaloe of Wrdisten that some have been led to suppose that there were two Winwaloes. Largillière's thesis[63] is that the *Vita Ethbini* is the work of a clerk of Montreuil. The story of the leper was invented by someone who knew that there were two saints honoured there called Ethbin and Winwaloe. We have seen that the *Vita Ethbini* mentions a certain Baumerus. Now close to Montreuil there is a parish called Beaumerie-Saint-Martin, the church of which is dedicated to S. Walloy (the Montreuil form of Winwaloe). The Hôtel-Dieu at Montreuil possesses a beautifully written *cueilloir* of 1477, and it is significant that the miniature at the head of the chapter of this book which deals with Beaumerie is a picture representing the miracle of the leper. It looks then, as if the church of S. Walloy at Beaumerie, about a mile from Montreuil, suggested the visit of Winwaloe and Ethbin to the chapel supposed to be at the same distance from "Taurac." The story,

[63] *Mélanges d'Hagiographie bretonne* (Brest, 1925).

perhaps first inserted into a book of miracles of saints connected with Montreuil, was appropriated for the *Vita Ethbini* and so passed into the *Vita Idiuneti* and finally became part of the later traditions of Landévennec. It was also taken from the *Vita Ethbini* and interpolated into the *Vita Winwaloei* by English clerks. Largillière's theory is exceedingly ingenious, but we are not obliged to follow him in supposing that Ethbin was really an Irish saint or had anything to do with Ireland. True, his Life says he went there, but states that he took up his abode in the *Silva que Nectensis dicitur*, which in reality is at Senlis. Duine thinks that the name *Ethbin* might be the same as that of *Etwin*, a youthful companion of the son of King Cadfan in Welsh legend.[64] It seems, too, impossible to follow Largillière when he suggests that the monks of Landévennec brought the *Vita Ethbini* back with them from Montreuil. This would not allow time enough for a story so different from the Landévennec tradition to grow up and afterwards be introduced into the *Vita Ethbini*, and for the latter to become acceptable to Landévennec monks who possessed and trusted Wrdisten's Life of Winwaloe.

The cartulary helps us again in the chapters 23 and 24, which describe the conversion of the sons of Catamaglus. Charter IX deals with *Roscatmagli* (now Roscanvel, on the narrow horn which runs out northward at the western end of the peninsula of Crozon), and quotes the story of three robbers in Wrdisten's Life.

Chapter 26 contains the most beautiful legend in the Life of S. Winwaloe. It is clearly an ancient tradition of Landévennec, and there is hardly a more charming story in the whole of Celtic hagiography. The story in c.27, on the other hand, is of the most commonplace kind.

The story of the saint's death in c.28 may be, as Duine suggests, imitated from similar stories in the *Vitae Patrum*. The Life of S. Cunval, as he points out, states that its hero, like Winwaloe, died at the altar, after receiving the sacred host and addressing a short exhortation to the congregation.[65]

§

[64] *Inventaire liturgique* . . ., p. 178. The chapel of S. Cadfan is near Pleyben.

[65] This study was finished before I had seen the article by H. Guiriec, entitled "Autour du Cartulaire de Landévennec," with two maps, in the *Bulletin de la Soc. Arch. du Finistère*, 1939, pp. 3-26. He considers Wrdisten's *Vita S. Winwaloei* to be a polemic against the centralizing measures of the Carolingian emperors, written in the reaction following the restoration of Breton independence by Nominoë, and thinks that his panegyrics of Winwaloe as the *eximius monachorum pater* may have been a protest against the enforced introduction of the Rule of S. Benedict.

It may seem to the reader disappointing to find that this lengthy ninth-century Life tells us in reality so little about S. Winwaloe. The only undoubted facts about him which it contains are his stay with S. Budoc on the island of Laurea and his foundation of the abbey of Landévennec, after a first essay on the island of Tibidy, together with the record of his ascetic habits, the day of the month on which he died and his burial in the little church of the monastery. Still, slender as the story is, yet, combined with what we know from other sources of the persons and places mentioned in it, it gives us the outline of several important chapters in the early history of the Church in Brittany.

The islands near Paimpol formed, until the French Revolution, an enclave of the diocese of Dol. Hagiographical writings like the *Vita Maudeti*, and the study of Breton and Cornish topography, show that on these islands were monasteries founded by S. Samson and his successors,[66] which contained important schools. Both S. Maudez and S. Budoc are described, in Cornwall and Brittany, as "masters." The most famous pupil of the latter was Winwaloe. His memory was cherished close to the place where he had for so long lived with Budoc—there was formerly a chapel of Saint Guénolé on the Île Beniguet.[67] Two other saints connected with Winwaloe (afterwards believed to be his brothers) were associated with the same group of monasteries—we have seen that the abbey of Saint-Jacut, the chief focus of the cult of S. Wethenoc and S. Jacobus, was an enclave of Dol. When he left Laurea, Winwaloe was first sent to a riverside monastery near Morlaix, still called after him *Locquenolé*,[68] which was another enclave of Dol. From there he was sent to found a monastery in Cornouaille. One of the things that most strikes the historian as he looks at the map of Cornouaille is the association of the cult of S. Winwaloe with that of S. Budoc. The church of S. Guénolé at Penmarch is near the church of Beuzec-Cap-Caval, which in the fourteenth century was the centre of a

[66] There was a chapel of S. Samson, now destroyed, on the Île de Bréhat.

[67] Mentioned in 1198 in the confirmation of the possessions of the abbey of Saint-Rion by Innocent III, now destroyed.

[68] *Locus Guennolay* in 1330. No. XXXVII in the cartulary describes a miracle worked by Winwaloe here "with water from the well which the Lord had given him there, *ubi postea monasteriolum fecerunt fratres in honore sancti Uuingualoei*." In 1163 the *ecclesia sancti Guingaloei* belonged to the abbey of Saint-Jacut.

deanery containing twenty-two parishes.[69] East of the Odet we find the parish church and priory of Concarneau, dedicated to S. Winwaloe and belonging to Landévennec, close to Beuzec-Conq, described in the cartulary (No. XIX) as *Locus sancti Uuingaloei in Buduc.* The cartulary mentions (No. XLI) *Bud Mael*, the form of S. Budoc's name found in the *Vita Maudeti* There is a chapel of S. Guénolé in Beuzec-Cap-Sizun.

But the foundation of Landévennec was not the only link between Cornouaille and the islands of the diocese of Dol near Paimpol. We have seen that Wrdisten distinctly states that Winwaloe had been preceded there by the monk Tutual, by whom, as I have shown, he means the founder of Loctudy, the other great monastery of Cornouaille. As the *Vita Maudeti* represents Bothmael (=Budoc) and Tudy as being Maudez' disciples, Wrdisten's statement exactly falls in with his description of Winwaloe as the disciple of Budoc and therefore belonging to the generation following Tudy.

But Winwaloe and Tudy were not the first Christian missionaries in Cornouaille. The place names in the Cartulary of Landévennec, so many of which begin with *Lan* and *Sent*, and the curious stories in Wrdisten and in the cartulary in which we find repeatedly a saint giving land to Winwaloe, show that the country was already full of churches and little monasteries.[70]

[69] M. Waquet, the archivist of Finistère, has pointed out to me the existence of a group of place-names in Cap Caval—St Guénolé, Beuzec, Plobannalec, Kerity—reproducing names in the Paimpol area. We have a similar phenomenon in Cornwall in the names of parishes in Penwith and Roseland.

[70] *Le Saint* near Gourin in south-east Cornouaille is exactly the same word as *Lezant* in Cornwall. In the cartulary it is *Lan Sent* and *Ecclesia Sanctus* (No. 24), while Lezant was *Lan Sant* in 1276. *Sant* was the name of the father of S. David. F. M. Duine has given (*Inv. Lit.*, pp. 53–6) a list of names associated with S. Winwaloe or with Landévennec, found in Wrdisten, in the cartulary, etc. I add it here for the sake of completeness, omitting those already dealt with: S. Berduualt, who gave himself and his possessions, viz. Lan Herprit and the *locus* called Lan Bertuualt, to S. Winwaloe (Cart. 25); S. Biabili, a hermit in Irvillac, disciple of S. Winwaloe (ib. 29); S. Conogan, a "confessor who had a spiritual colloquy with S. Winwaloe concerning the salvation of his soul" and gave him Beuzec-Saint-Conogan near Landerneau *usque ad visionem claustri sancti Huardon* (Cart. 41, which is of special interest). The relics of S. Conogan were taken to Montreuil (Duine, *Mém.*, No. 129. See the index to Rodière's *Les Corps saints de Montreuil*); S. Edern (Cart., 46), evidently a Welsh saint. There is a Llanedern in the deanery of Llandaff (the parish contains a *Llangadog*) and another in the deanery of Lleyn in Carnarvonshire. There is a *Bodedern* in Holyhead. (*Inv. Lit.*, p. 53, note 7); S. Enéour (Cart. 1 and 47, see Loth, *Noms*, p. 38); S. Gourdelou, eponym of a small *lan* at Beuzit-Saint-Conogan (Cart.41); S. Houardon (see above); S. Iglur (Cart. 22, *Noms*, p. 64); S. Ilian, whose name comes between those of Conogan and Houardon in the Litany of Salisbury; S. Jud, abbot of Landévennec (*Inv. Lit.*, p. 53, note 2); S. Martin, disciple of S. Winwaloe, hermit at Irvillac (Cart. 29); S. Morbret (Cart. 39. See my "S. Meubred, Cardynham," pp. 5–7); S. Ratian (Cart. 22),

continued on next page

Our study of Wrdisten's *Vita Winwaloei* and of the cartulary of Landévennec and other documents contained in MS.16 in the Library of Quimper seems, then, to have led us to the discovery of some important facts. The chief event in the story of the organization of the Celtic church in Cornwall and Brittany was the coming of Samson with a band of monks and evangelists from South Wales to Dol. One of the most important of their works was the establishment of monasteries with famous schools on the islands at the entrance of the Bay of Saint-Brieuc. From them the two chief monasteries of Cornouaille were founded, one of which absorbed many of the older Christian settlements in the west of Brittany. There was evidently also a close connection betweeen the island monasteries of Paimpol and the south coast of Devon and Cornwall, where we find churches dedicated to Sampson, Maudez, Budoc, Tudy, Corentin and Winwaloe.

§

It remains to examine the cult of S. Winwaloe, the place he occupies in ancient liturgical books and the churches dedicated in his honour.

His name is found in the kalendars of every one of the nine ancient dioceses of Brittany, and in those of the abbeys of Saint-Méen[71] and of Saint-Melaine-de-Rennes.[72] He is invoked, with S. Corentin, in the tenth-century Litany of Salisbury, in that of the Psalter of Rheims,[73] both of English origin and both composed for Breton clerks exiled in England,[74] and also in the Litany of Limoges (eleventh century)—again with S. Corentin.[75] We have

[71] Duine, *Inventaire liturgique . . .*, p. 199.
[72] ib. p. 70, cf. 158.
[73] ib. p. 47.
[74] ib. p. 45.
[75] ib., pp. 59, 60.

---

continued from previous page

who gave his lands, including Lan Ratian, at Coray to S. Winwaloe *propter cladem suae gentis*. His *locus* was consequently preserved from the pestilence; S. Tanuoud gave land to S. Winwaloe (Cart. 16); S. Tydecho, eponym of *Lan Decheuc*, given by S. Morbret to S. Winwaloe (Cart. 39). In late Welsh genealogies he is a brother of S. Samson (see Duine, *Mém.*, No. 118); S. Warhen, butler of King Gradlon, in whose house the king held a council at which Winwaloe and Corentin were present (Cart. 20), eponym of Busitt Sent Uuarhen in Pleyben (Cart. 33); S. Wengu (see my *Children of Brychan*, pp. 13-14); Near her famous well is a village of S. Guénolé (*Inv. Lit.* p. 56, note 33); S. Wicon (Cart. No. 12); S. Wiwret, whose *lan* was given to Landévennec (Cart. 38, *Noms*, p. 40); S. Wrguestle (Cart. 10). In Cornwall we find the name *Wurguistel* (*uur* or *gour* = "man," *gwystel* = "pledge" or "hostage") in the manumissions in the Bodmin Gospels.

seen why he was honoured in the abbey of Saint-Jacut,[76] why he is invoked in the Litany of St-Vougay (in Léon)[77] and why his name appears in the liturgical books of churches on or near the Loire,[78] near Le Mans,[79] and in the neighbourhood of Montreuil.[80] His name is in the kalendars of Saint-Germain-des-Prés and of S. Marcel at Paris (the latter shows Montreuil influence; *Ethbin, confessor*, appears in the kalendar on October 19 and is invoked in the litany). [Winwaloe's name appears in the litany on S. Mark's day in the *Ordinale* of Saint-Vedast abbey at Arras].

Of special interest are the gospel-book and kalendar of the abbey of Landévennec. Three copies of the former (the contents of each being practically the same) have come down to us, as I have said already. One, written in a tenth-century hand, is now in the Bodleian Library at Oxford (MS. Auct. D.2.16). For the *Natale sancti Uuinualoi* the gospel is Matt. 24:42-47, that for the *Translatio beati Uuinualoi confessoris* (Apr. 28) is Luke 19:12-26. For the *Dedicatio Basilice sancti Guingualoi confessoris* on May 13 we find Luke 6:43-48. This book once belonged to Leofric, first bishop of Exeter, who gave it to Exeter cathedral, and who made some additions for its use there, including a list of the relics (among them relics of S. Winwaloe[81]) given to the monastery at Exeter, mostly by Athelstan but some perhaps by Leofric himself. Here we clearly have the reason for our saint being invoked in the very long list of saints in the Litany of the Leofric Collectar, where Sancte Winuualoe comes after Sancte Neote

[76] ib. p. 146.

[77] Duine, *Saints de Domnonée*, p. 40.

[78] Duine, *Inv. Lit.*, pp. 36, 73, 81, 104.

[79] Fifteenth-cent. Breviary of Le Mans, March 3, *Guingaloy, abbatis Landevennech.* Duine, *Inv. Lit.*, pp. 97, 113, 114. An early fragment of a martyrology from the Barberini Library, now at the Vatican, which seems to come from Maine (perhaps from Saint-Calais) has "Cornubiae natale sancti Guingualoei confessoris" under IIII kal. Maii and "Cornubiae natale sancti Courentini confessoris atque pontificis" under kal. Maii (See H. Quentin, *Les Martyrologes historiques*, pp. 32 and 33).

[80] In a Ghent martyrology "At the monastery of Blandin at Ghent the memory of blessed Winvualieu, abbot," under March 3 (the abbey claimed to possess his relics); at Cambrai a fifteenth-century collection of lives of saints has a *Vita Winwoloci*, and a fourteenth-century manuscript from the abbey of Loos near Lille has short Lives of Etbin and Winwaloe on f. 51; a martyrology of the abbey of Saint-Riquier (in the eleventh-century crypt of which were relics of our saint) contains his name (*Inv. Lit.*, pp. 14, 24, 74).

[81] *Reliquiae Winuualoi confessoris* (Leofric Missal, p. 5, ed. Warren). In the list in the gospel-book, written in Anglo-Saxon, the entry is *Of S. Winwaloe tham abbode*. It is to be observed that among the Exeter relics are those of several other saints honoured at Montreuil, *e.g.* Conocan, Macutus, Wlmar and Wolfran. E. W. B. Nicholson says (*Introduction to Some of the Oldest Latin Musical MSS. in the Bodleian*), "it was executed in the 10th century at Landévennec (after the re-migration) to be sent to Montreuil, and . . . . brought to England by Leofric."

and before Sancte Maucanne and Sancte Gilda. "Et sci. wynwaloci conf." has been added in the kalendar of the Leofric Missal on April 28. There were also relics of S. Winwaloe at Glastonbury,[82] and relics of Winwaloe and *Caurentin* (given by Athelstan) at Abingdon. A manuscript at the British Museum (Harley 3776) gives a list of the relics at Waltham Abbey in the middle ages: they had *Reliqu. de sco Winwaleo. i de sco. Courentino*, but of no other Celtic saints except S. Petroc and S. Nectan.

The Kalendar of Landévennec is in the Royal Library of Copenhagen (handwriting of eleventh century): the last four months of the year are missing. The names of *S. Winvaloeus* on March 3 (*Depositio*) and April 28 (*in Cornu Galliae, Translatio*), of S. Patrick and of *S. Courentin* are in large letters. The kalendar contains some English saints (Cuthbert, Etheldreda and Augustine) In the *computum*, against the year 913 or 914, are the words "Eodem anno destructum est monasterium Sancti Winvaloei a Normannis."

A list of churches and chapels in France where S. Winwaloe is patron will be found to mark, first, his passage from the Île de Lavrea, by Locquenolé, to Landévennec; secondly, the gradual extension of the property owned by the abbey; and thirdly, the journeyings of his relics till they found a permanent home at Montreuil. With the first group of dedications we must join two in Léon. One is that of the chapel at Lesven in Plouguin. The other is the dedication of the church of Saint-Frégant to S. Guénolé. The name of the parish apparently commemorates, as we have seen, his father Fracan, and there is a holy well of S. Guénolé there, ornamented with a carving representing the story of Chreirbia and the gander. There seems to have been a tradition about Winwaloe's family in the north-west of Léon, unknown to or ignored by Wrdisten, but very familiar to Albert Le Grand, who has improved on it in his usual manner at the beginning of his *Vie de S. Guennolé*.

Another dedication to S. Winwaloe (which has never, I think, been noticed before), of about the same early date but far removed on the map from the dedications of northern Brittany, is found at Auville in Normandy (near Carentan, in the Côtentin), where the patron saint is *S. Guingalais*. It is to be observed that the parish is very near the "Exemption de Ste-Mère-Eglise"—an

[82] Hearne's edition (1726) of John of Glastonbury's *Chronica* . . ., pp. 449, 451.

enclave of five parishes belonging to the diocese of Bayeux, which seems to be a survival of a former monastery of S. Mewan (the cousin of S. Samson), as to which written records are silent. Ste-Mère-Eglise is dedicated to S. Méen. There is a statue of S. Winwaloe (locally pronounced *Guingaloué*) in the church of Auville (which is no longer a separate parish). (See Seguin, *Les traditions populaires dans la Basse Normandie.*)

We have seen that the church of the monastery of Landévennec was the *Basilica Sancti Guingualoi*. Wrdisten's Life gives us some most precious details about the exact position of the monastery in his day, which helps us to picture it, with its enclosing wall, its one entrance, facing east, reached by a circuitous and narrow approach, its cemetery and its church, and it has preserved the traditional stories about its foundation and the twice-repeated change of site; but, apart from the "precept" of Louis le Débonnaire ordering the introduction of the Rule of S. Benedict, and a few details like the reference to the replacing of the original small Celtic church by a larger one, it does not tell us much about the history of the abbey. The cartulary has a number of traditions on the subject, mostly of a legendary character, and it is to be noted that it does not give us the names of any abbots before Matmonoch, except those of S. Winwaloe and S. Guenaël (by tradition his successor).

Wrdisten does not name his monastery, though he has preserved the imperial "precept" in which it is called monasterium *Landeuinnoch*. He himself refers to it as *Monasterium Sancti Winwaloei*. The cartulary has "Ego Gradlonus rex veni usque *Lanteguennoc*" (No. 23), *Lanteuuennuc* (28), and "Uuenlouen . . . cupiebat videre locum sancti Uuingualoei qui vocatur *Lanteuuennoc*" (36). Scholars differ as to the signification of the name. All are agreed that it means "The Monastery of Wennoc," whose name is preceded by the *to* or *te* common in the hypocoristic form of Celtic saints' names, which becomes *de* after *lan*. Thus in Wales S. Sulian is commonly called Tysilio, and he is the eponym of five places called Landysilio. In Cornwall we have Towednack (the eponym being S. Tewynnoc), Landewednack and Landegea (the eponym of the later being S. Ké), and in Brittany St Thegonnec.[83] This *to* (which corresponds to an Irish *mo*) is variously interpreted as an honorific prefix, a demonstrative (this was

[83] He is the "Quonocus quem alii sub additamento more gentis transmarinae Toquonocum vocant" (Wrmonoc's *Vita Pauli Aureliani*).

Loth's opinion), or a possessive adjective of the second person.[84]

Loth saw in *de Wennoc* a hypocoristic form of the name *Winwaloe*, and M. Vendryes follows him. Largillière regarded this as very doubtful. He says[85] that the expression in Charter 36 of the cartulary (quoted above), "the *locus* of S. Wingualoaeus which is called Lanteuuennoc" suggests that "the monks were entirely ignorant of the meaning of the place-name; the original abbey or *lan* had been ruined and abandoned, though its name remained, and later a *locus* or monastery of S. Winwaloe had been built on its site."

It seems to me possible that the name may really mean "The Lan of S. Wethnoc," The abbey owned a place in Pleyben called *Lan Uuethnoc* (Cart. 33). In Cornwall, where there is a parish whose name begins with *Lan*, the church is hardly ever dedicated to the eponym of the *lan*. There are a good many dedications in Brittany to a S. *Guennec*. He is the eponym of Trevenneuc and of Lanvignec (an enclave of Dol near Paimpol) in the C.-du-N.; of *Saint-Venoc* in Plouhinec (west of Quimper), of *Saint-Vennec* in Combrit (south-west of Quimper), in Briec (north of Quimper) and in Landrevarzec (where the parish church is dedicated to S. Winwaloe); and of *Lanvenec* in Plourin and in Lanrivoaré (the latter place is spelt *Lan-guenoc* in the cartulary, No. 39, and is described as "the heritage of S. Guenaël"). Now at Saint-Vennec in Briec the tradition was that the saint was the same as S. Weithnoc, brother of Winwaloe, for there is a statue in the chapel representing Alba Trimammis with Winwaloe on her knees and Weithnoc and Jacut at her side. This Weithnoc, as I have said, was evidently an important person in ancient Breton ecclesiastical tradition. It is significant that Exeter cathedral possessed, together with the relics of S. Winwaloe, some *de corpore Withenoci confessoris*. It is also to be observed that S. Winwaloe was the patron of a chapel at Quemper-*Guezennec* (C.-du-N.). Winwaloe and Wethnoc must have been closely associated with each other, though the Life of the former does not tell us anything about the latter except that he was a brother, and has no story of their being together in after years. In Cornwall a S. Wethinoc plays a very important part in the Life of S. Petroc; he was the eponym

[84] See Vendryes, *Sur les hypocoristiques celtiques précédés de TO* (*Etudes Celtiques*, Dec., 1937, pp. 254f.).

[85] *Op. cit.*, p. 42, n. 81.

of Landuvethnoc (the old name of Padstow). William of Worcester found his name in the kalendar of Bodmin Priory on November 7, and, as Guethnoc was honoured at Saint-Jacut on November 5 and the name *In Brit. Gueutnoci conf.* appears in a sacramentary of the north of France on November 11, it seems as if the Cornish and Breton Wethenocs were the same person. Mr Henderson also saw the name Guethenoc in *Lanuthinoc*, the name of St Erth in 1200. Duine regards *Weithnoc* and *Guennec* as the same name.

A large number of the places mentioned in the cartulary still have (or had until the Revolution) churches or chapels dedicated in honour of S. Winwaloe. Thus he is the patron of the parish churches of Bourg de Batz near Guérande (Cart. 25), of the Ile de Sein (Cart. 5), of Landrévarzec, with a chapel at Treflez, now in Briec. (Cart 13), of Concarneau[86] (Cart. 19), and of Edern (Cart. 16).

He is the patron of chapels at Gourin (with a pardon; Cart. 19), at Langonnet (Cart. 19), at Clohars-Fouesnant (? Cart. 43), and at Gouezec (now destroyed, but the holy well of S. Guénolé still exists; Cart.17). There are chapels dedicated to him at Penmarch, Plougastel-Daoulas, Ergué-Gaberic, Lopérec,[87] Plogoff, Locronan, Ouessant, Crozon, Pleyben, Quéménéven (near Saint-Vennec in Briec), Scaër, Pluguffan, Collorec (north-east of Pleyben),[88] Quimperlé, Bannalec, Mellac, Riec, Moëlan, Querrien (all near Quimperlé), Poldreuzic, Beuzec-Cap-Sizun (west of Quimper), Pleuven, Elliant, and Coray near Quimper, and two chapels at Plonevez-Porzay (at Lanzent and at Kerleau). He has chapels at Lannillis and Carantec in Léon. There is a *Loquenolé* in Plounevez-du-Faou, and a *Locunolé* near Querrien (north of Quimperlé) and another at Le Faouet (*aveu* of 1684.)

In the department of the Côtes-du-Nord he has chapels at

[86] He was patron, not only of the priory, but of the parish church. The latter has been recently destroyed, and the new one dedicated in honour of the Holy Heart of Mary, which seems a pity. *Guénolé* was, I believe, a favourite name for boys at Concarneau. A. Le Grand says S. Guénolé was the patron of the whole town.

[87] For the history of the chapel of S. Guénolé in Lopérec see *Bull. d'Hist. et. d'Arch. du diocèse de Quimper*, 1928, pp. 250–3, 308, 311. There seems to be a connection between S. Petroc and both Winwaloe and Jacut.

[88] The saint's chapel and holy well at Collorec are described by Anatole Le Braz (*Les Saints bretons d'après la tradition populaire en Cornouaille*, 1937. pp. 83–6), who relates a tradition that the saint was fond of going to dances when a boy, and that his first miracle was the detention of his father's poultry in a grange without doors for a whole evening, so that he might go to the dance. The pardon was on the 1st Sunday in October, and dances were held on Pardon Monday.

Plourac'h (near Callac), Tonquedec (near Lannion), Trévou-Tréguignec on the coast near Perros-Guirec (the parish church is dedicated to S. Samson and the parish was an enclave of Dol), Ploumiliau, Quemper-Guezennec (destroyed, there was also a chapel of S. Samson in the latter parish) and Merléac (near Quintin). He has a statue at Saint-Jacut-de-Plestin and Squiffiec. The dedications to St Guénolé in the diocese of Vannes are all grouped in the south-west: viz. Locunolé in Inzinzac, Pontscorff, Kervignac, Quistinic and Priziac.[89]

We have seen that S. Winwaloe is the patron of the church of Château-du-Loir near Le Mans, and that this probably indicates the resting-place of his body on its way to Montreuil. It was evidently an important centre of his cult, and kept in touch with Cornouaille. Another resting-place may have been at Pierric, in Brittany but on the border of Anjou, where he is the patron of the church. S. Guénolé is patron of the town of Croisic in the diocese of Nantes. The churches of Saint-Laud and Saint-Serge in Angers claimed to possess some of his relics.

The monks of Landévennec were warmly welcomed at Montreuil. Count Helgaud, we read in a charter of Abbot Rameric in the year 1000, "received them with honour and showed them even greater honour by giving them a permanent home." They were a large party, for besides their abbot Benedict (the predecessor of John) they had numbers of clerks and brethren with them, and the count, Rameric tells us, gave them the *villa* of Cavron, that they might live on its revenues and that their lay-brethren might dwell there. A charter of King Henry I of France, dated 1042, recalls the reception of "the aforesaid saint, brought from the parts of Brittany for fear of the pirates," and adds the interesting fact that the monks were first lodged in "a public *atrium* in the cemetery reserved for strangers and pilgrims, and afterwards the count gave them nine houses below the castle, with the adjoining meadow. Finally he added to his gifts the *villa* of Cavron . . . with its two churches and its mills." One of these churches was afterwards rededicated to S. Winwaloe. At a later date the *villa* of Beaumerie was given to the abbey, and its church was also rededicated to S. Winwaloe, becoming *altare Sancti Winvaloei de Belmery*.[90]

[89] It will be remembered that it was at Priziac that Matmonoc had his interview with the emperor (Life, bk. II, c. 12).

[90] Rodière, *Les Corps saints de Montreuil* (1901), pp. 8–10, 49.

The body of S. Winwaloe was placed in the church of the abbey of Saint-Sauve and regarded with great veneration. So great was the interest aroused at Montreuil by the coming of the monastic community of Landévennec that the abbey changed its name and for nearly two centuries was known as the Abbey of Saint-Walloy. Abbot Rameric, in the charter quoted above, calls himself "a humble minister of the church of the blessed Winwaloe of Montreuil." and the charter is dated "in coenobio Sti. Winwaloei apud castrum Monsterolum." About this time the monks, to avoid having the parochial services in their abbey church, built a parish church within the monastic enclosure. The parish of Saint-Walloy continued to exist down to the French Revolution, when it was suppressed, together with all the other parishes of the town, and the abbey church made parochial.[91] On S. Winwaloe's feast on April 28 the shrine[92] containing his body was carried by the monks singing *Iste confessor* in procession from the abbey to Saint-Walloy parish church, at 5-30 a.m., preceded by the curé and his clergy.[93] The shrine was left at Saint-Walloy till after Vespers, when it was fetched back in the same way. On the Sunday following it was carried in procession, preceded by the mayor and *échevins* and the banners of the corporations and guilds, to a field called *La Fosse Saint-Walloy* in the parish of Saint-Justin outside the town. After a sermon there by a preacher appointed by the monks of Saint-Sauve it was brought back with the same ceremonial.[94]

Processions carrying the shrines of the ten saints whose relics were preserved at Montreuil (the parishioners of Saint-Walloy carried his shrine) formed a principal part of the public life of the town. The Processional of the abbey (1753) describes those held

[91] This church was a "bijou de sculpture gothique." Some fragments of its carvings are now preserved in the garden of the Hôtel de Longvilliers: "there is nothing in the whole neighbourhood comparable to them for perfect finish and delicacy of detail" (ib. p. 49, note 1). It was demolished in 1793. Its site is at the bottom of an *impasse* south-west of the abbey, still called the Place Saint-Valloy.

[92] In 1495 the shrine was in a state of decay, and a new one of wood covered with silver, 3½-ft. long, 2-ft. high and 1-ft. wide, with scenes from the life of the saint on it, was made. The bishop of Amiens presided over the solemn translation of the saint's body into it. He found in the old one an ancient label with the words RELIQUIAE SANCTI WINWALOEI CONFESSORIS ET ABBATIS (ib. 80-2).

[93] Before removing the shrine the following anthem was sung:

> "O Pater Winvaloee, dulcis in memoria,
> Sed cum Christo jam perenni dulcior in gloria,
> Quibus ipse jucundaris inter coeli vernulas,
> Fac ut ad coelestis regni admittamur epulas. Alleluia."

followed by versicle, response and collect.

[94] Rodière, *op. cit.*, p. 57.

on Palm Sunday, April 28, Ascension day and the Sunday following, Whitmonday, Corpus Christi and the Sunday following, and on the Assumption. When the treasury containing the shrines was opened, on Whitsun eve and in times of public calamity, special anthems, etc. were chanted before every one of the shrines.[95] M. Roduère gives a detailed description of the destruction of all the shrines and relics at Saint-Sauve on Sept. 30, 1793.

There were important relics of saints in the abbey of Saint-Sauve, including those of Corentin, Conogan, Ethbin and Machutus (Malo). But Winwaloe held the first place in popular estimation. The monks had brought from Landévennec, besides his body, the bell, chasuble and alb which the saint had used. In 1664 Jacques de Bove, curé of Saint-Walloy and canon of Saint-Firmin, sent to Henschenius, the successor of Bollandus, a copy of all the documents about S. Winwaloe which the monks could find, together with drawings of the bell and vestments and small fragments of all the relics. The Bollandists printed descriptions of these in the *Acta Sanctorum* (March, vol. i, p. 248, Paris edition). The size of the alb and of the bones showed that the saint must have been a very tall man. The chasuble was of the original round shape, large and full, the alb was of cotton, both were in a marvellous state of preservation (but they may have been renewed). The bell was a small one, almost black in colour; it was called *Campanula Sti Winwaloei*, and was "held in veneration by the people."[96] It had made a great impression on the people of Montreuil from the first. As both Montreuil and Landévennec are on the sea, and the Life of the saint has a good deal about the sea in it, the idea arose that Winwaloe used the bell to attract fish, and in ancient statues and paintings at Montreuil and the neighbourhood he is invariably represented holding the bell in his right hand and usually the abbatial staff in his left, with three fishes rising out of the sea beneath the bell in obedience to his summons.[97] The *Vita*, it will be remembered, states that

[95] ib. pp. xvii, 123–130, 326–335, 377.

[96] ib. pp. 133–5.

[97] At the abbey there was a statue of S. Walloy among the fourteen fine figures placed in the west porch there in 1470; the lower part of it (the only part which escaped mutilation in 1793) is now in the museum at Boulogne. A similar representation of the saint is found on the funerary bas-relief of Abbot Guillaume de La Pasture (1504) in the abbey church. There are two ancient statues of the saint with his bell and the fish in the church at Cavron, which once possessed a bell called after the saint, given in 1631. In the inscription on it appear the words +WALOIS MA NOMME. It is now in the church of Galway in Ireland. (See Rodière, p. 134, note 3, p. 49, note 3).

fish formed an important part of the saint's diet. But the idea that fishes listened to his bell is unknown in Brittany and is only found at Montreuil.

From Montreuil the cult of S. Winwaloe spread to Flanders. The abbey of Mont-Blandin at Ghent claimed to possess his relics, and that of Marchiennes possessed his Life. There were also Lives of S. Winwaloe at the abbeys of Anchin and Rouge-Cloître in Belgium. Thence too the knowledge of our saint reached Canterbury and other places in England. In the city of Norwich there is still a *St Winwaloe Street*, where once was a church of the saint, given by King Stephen to the nuns of Carrow and re-dedicated to S. Katherine. Wareham Priory, near Stoke Ferry in Norfolk, founded at the end of the twelfth century, a cell of Montreuil, was dedicated to him, and there is an East Anglian proverb which shows that his festival in March was once well-known there:

> "First comes David, then comes Chad,
> Then comes Winnol, as if he were mad,"

meaning that the first three days in March are usually stormy.

Baring-Gould and Fisher (*Lives of the British Saints*, vol. iv, p. 36) declare Winwaloe to be the patron of Wonastow near Monmouth, but there seem to be no grounds for this. In the Book of Llandaff, Wonastow is *Lanngunguarui*. Nor is there any question of the cult of a Breton saint being introduced here after the Norman Conquest, as in Norfolk, for the patron is given as *Saint Wengel* in 1254. "St Twinells" in Pembrokeshire was *Ecclesia S. Winnoci* in 1291.

THE CULT OF S. WINWALOE IN CORNWALL AND DEVON

The cult of S. Winwaloe in Cornwall is quite independent of the influence of Montreuil and goes back to the Age of the Saints. It seems, however, certain that it was brought from Brittany. Latouche indeed suggested that Winwaloe might be "a pan-Celtic saint whose cult was imported from Cornwall into Brittany." But there are serious objections to this view. It contradicts all the traditions we possess about the saint. It would make his cult an extremely early one, and we have seen that it appears on the contrary to be a late cult, superseding that of other older saints in Léon and Cornouaille. It seems impossible, when we compare the two places, that Landewednack should be the mother of Landévennec. The former is a tiny village in barren land on a very exposed and dangerous coast, and can never have been an important place. The latter is in a superb position on one of the finest land-locked harbours in the world. It was the principal religious centre of the west of Brittany, having numerous smaller monasteries under its jurisdiction. One of these was probably Landewednack. The site of the church, in a sheltered hollow just above a little landing-place called Church Cove, was clearly chosen because of the advantages it possessed for quick communication by water with some other large settlement.

It is remarkable that, while Wrdisten refers to no traditions of foundations by Winwaloe outside Brittany, the Life of Guenaël tells us that the latter saint, who succeeded Winwaloe as abbot of Landévennec, "founded in greater Britain and in Ireland, by miracles and apostolic labour, two famous monasteries, and afterwards others to the number of fifty."[98] The Life, which is a short one, does not name them nor tell us exactly where they were (nor does it name the three monasteries which it goes on to say he founded in Cornouaille on his return), but Cornwall is as likely a site for them as any. The statement proves at any rate the existence of a tradition that he visited this country and may explain at least some of the Cornish dedications to Winwaloe. In this connection it is interesting to note that the Cartulary of Landévennec tells us that Languennoc in Léon was "the inheritance of Saint Uuenhael" (No. 39). It is possible that he may have given a similar name to a *lan* in Cornwall and have dedicated its church to his saintly predecessor.

Apart from the *Vita Guenaili*, there is no documentary evidence whatever as to the origin of the cult of S. Winwaloe in Cornwall, and we are left to depend entirely on the evidence of place-names and church dedications.

LANDEWEDNACK. The name of the parish of Landewednack presents a phenomenon almost unique in this period—the transference, not merely of the cult of a saint (which is, of course, exceedingly common) but of a place-name as well.

[98] *Acta Sanctorum*, November, vol. i, p. 676.

As is usual in Cornwall, the *lan* bears the name of one saint while the church is dedicated to another. At Towednack, on the other hand, where there is no *lan*, the church is dedicated to "S. Tewennoc the Confessor" (1409), who is called in 1516 simply "Wennack."

The following are the different names of the parish found in ancient records. (The manor of *Lusart* is named in Domesday, but the parish itself is not mentioned before the thirteenth century.)

Ecclesia Sancti Wynwolay (1290, Taxation of Pope Nicholas).
Landewennec, 1310.
Ecc. Sci. Wynwolayi de Lanwynnocke, 1314.
Ecc. Sci. Wynwolay de Landewenecke, 1336.
Landwynecke juxta Lesarde, 1385.

In 1541 James Erisey left 3/4 to *St Gunwall in Tyrar* (*i.e., in Terra Arida*, the latter being a soubriquet for this district—Ruan Minor is so described in 1447).

The advowson of the Church of Gunwallowe, 1555.
Goenwallowe alias Landawenocke, 1582.

This was one of the churches on the great fee of Richard de Luci in the twelfth century (called sometimes, after him, "Lucie's," but generally *Rosuic*, from the barton in St Keverne). John de Ripariis, lord of the fee, was patron in 1278. From 1349 the patronage was in the Carminow family.

The most striking feature of the church is its serpentine tower of the fifteenth century. The church has a Norman doorway, and porch and windows of the fourteenth century, a font bearing the name of Richard Bolham, Rector 1404-1415, a large passage squint and several features peculiar to the churches of the Lizard district.

There is an ancient cross at the head of the lane leading down to the church; the adjacent field is called, after it, Parc Growes. There were formerly at least three other crosses in the parish, as the field-names *Parkengrouse* (No. 231, in South Trethvas), *Parkgrouse* (404, in Tregominion Wollas) and *Crosswidden* (=White Cross, in Trenoweth) show. A cross over a grave in the churchyard came from Merthen in Constantine, and the little gothic gable cross on the wall from Ruan Major church. There is no mention of any ancient chapels in the parish. "St Hellena" is probably a modern name, though found in 1840.

An interesting document in the Public Record Office, never printed before, explains the northern boundary of the parish. At Ruan Major, on Thursday the feast of the Assumption 1325, a declaration was made of the bounds of the moor of the lord of Tredeves, situate within the limits and tithings (*decimaciones*) of the parish of S. Wynwolaus of Landewennech, by Richard, vicar of the church of S. Melan (Mullion), John le Yorl, Edw: le Yorl, Richard le Oen, Henry le Oen, Odo de Landewennech, Wm. le Duer, John Wendreth and Richard David being sworn, and Thomas Marsily and John de Herysy, to whom the oath was remitted by the consent of Sir John Lonedrein (rector of Landewennech) and Master Matthew de Penfern, rector of S. Rumon Parvus, which rectors the present business concerned. They declared that the manor was thus bounded:

> On the west in a place called *Penkennans* (*i.e.*, The head of Kynance) and thence to Halmur, and thence to the moor of Predannechwartha, and thence to the stone called *Hyrven*, and thence by the sanctuary (=glebe) of Merther to the bridge of Merther and so outside the close of Pulkenow to the road dividing the moor from the moor of John Marsily of S. Rumon, and so by the road to Krucgrageth, and so by the road to the land of Gos (?). The road from Helston to Krucgrageth has a moor on the west of it, which is in the parish of Landewennech, and there is another part on the east side reaching to Ponsmerther: fifty years since Sir Henry Yyrel, rector of Landewennech, sent his servant to seek tithes at Ponsmerther. Nevertheless we consider it to belong to S. Ruan Parvus.

GUNWALLOE. This parish was one of the three chapelries of Breage. In ancient documents it is generally called *Winnianton*, from the very important royal manor, which in Domesday gives its name to the whole hundred. The site of the manor house is north of the church. The name of this ancient manor might be explained, Mr Henderson thought, by the fact that there was a Breton saint called *Guinien*, original patron of Ploudaniel in Léon (Loth, *Noms*, p. 57).

The church is dedicated to S. Winwaloe, and the church and parish are now called Gunwalloe, but before the seventeenth century they were always called after the name of the manor, and in medieval and sixteenth-century documents "Gunwalloe" always refers to Landewednack. This fact explains the Cornish vernacular form of the saint's name, for the great moor (in Cornish *gun* or *woon*) called Goonhilly Downs has clearly, by a false analogy, corrupted the first syllable of the saint's name at Landewednack. In the seventeenth century Landewednack ceased to be called Gunwalloe, and the name was transferred to the church of S. Winwaloe at Winianton.

Gunwalloe church is most beautifully situated on a little sandy creek, nestling against a great rock which completely hid it from pirates visiting Mount's Bay. Its romantic situation has given rise to romantic but groundless legends. It was rebuilt in the fifteenth century, but has a fragment of the Norman font. Parts of the rood screen erected when the church was rebuilt, or soon after, with apostles painted on the panels, remain, and also some of the carved roofing. The little tower, perfectly plain, is detached, and built into the rock. When Richard, earl of Cornwall, the lord of the manor, gave Breage church to Hailes Abbey in Gloucestershire in 1246, Cury and Gunwalloe chapels went with it.

There was a holy well underneath the churchyard wall on the south-western side. There has been much coast erosion here, and for a long time the sea has covered its site at every high tide, filling it with sand and shingle. Thomas Quiller Couch visited it in the second half of the nineteenth century, and wrote, "that this well was once considered by the country folk of some importance is plain, for one day in the year, called *Gunwalloe Day*, was set apart for cleaning out the holy well, a ceremony attended with much festive merriment. The festival, which differed in date from the Parish Feast (kept on the last Sunday in April), has been discontinued for many years, and lives only in the memories of two of the oldest men in the parish."[99]

In 1433 Sir John Arundell, Knight, left four marks to "the Store of the Chapel of S. Wynwola juxta Carminow." The names of some of the clergy serving this church have been recorded. Martin was *capellanus de Wynhampton* c.1410, and in 1449 Ralph Harry was chaplain of *Wynaton*. In 1537 this little church still had its own priest (the churches of Cornwall had a large staff of clergy before the Reformation).

Sowanna in this parish was formerly called *Saint Sowanna*

[99] *Ancient and Holy Wells of Cornwall* (1894), p. 79.

(*Seynt Sewanna* 1380, *Sissewana* 1500, *Saint Sewannowe* 1583). North-east of the farm buildings are two fields (numbered 332 and 334 on the parish map) called "Great and Little Parc-en-Chapel." Two other fields are called *Venton-Aram* (Nos. 338, 339). Who was the S. Sewanna who once had a chapel here?

TREMAINE. Mr Henderson thought that the dedication of this church in North Cornwall to S. Winwaloe might possibly be accounted for by the fact that William de Botrell, lord of Penhele, who granted the chapels of Egloskery, *Tremene* and Clakhampton (*i.e.*, St Gennys) to Launceston Priory, between 1150 and 1176, was a Breton.[100] From this time Egloskerry and Tremaine remained appropriated to Launceston Priory and were served together by one chaplain. It may be remarked that both these churches possess twelfth-century sculptured tympana by the same craftsman, and fonts resembling each other and of the same date. The name Tremaine is a secular one, meaning the *Stone Town*. Early in the sixteenth century the inhabitants obtained rights of burial. In September 1506 a petition was presented to the bishop by Robert Brode, Wm. Yolton, John Wasse and John Walys, parishioners of the "Capella Parochialis et Curata Sancti Winwolai de Tremene," stating that their chapelry had its own boundaries, that the parishioners maintained the fabric, while the priory provided at its own cost the chaplain who ministered there all the sacraments (except burial) which were ministered by him at the chapel of S. Keria at Egloskerry, that some of the parishioners lived four miles from the chapel, and the roads were recently become excessively bad, so that funerals at Egloskerry were a real hardship. They accordingly asked the bishop to consecrate their chapel and cemetery. After an inquiry, at which all the parties concerned were represented, Bishop Oldham issued a commision (16 Sept., 1506) to his suffragan John, Bishop of Sebaste (Samaria), to consecrate the *capella sancti Winwolai de Tremene et cimiterium ejusdem*. The *Composicio* drawn up on this occasion stipulated:

(1) That the Prior and Convent maintain a chaplain, who is to reside at Egloskery as formerly, and serve the chapel of S. Keria de Egloskery on alternate Sundays as of old custom.

[100] This is only a suggestion, for which there is no absolute proof. The three dedications to S. Winwaloe in East Cornwall are in a line running north from the ancient abbey-bishopric of Lanalet, now St Germans, which may have been visited by S. Guenaël.

(2) That provision be made for services at Tremaine on various feasts, including the two feasts of S. Winwolaus.

(3) That the tithes belonging to the altarage be offered before the image of S. Winwolaus, and 12d. and a candle of 1-lb. of wax offered in the priory church at Launceston before the beginning of high Mass on the morrow of Christmas (S. Stephen's day) as a sign of subjection. The candle shall burn before the image of S. Stephen.

Since this church belonged to the priory, the canons observed the feast of S. Winwaloe in their church. *Sancti Winwaloi abbatis* is entered in their kalendar on April 28.

ROSCRADDOCK In St Cleer. At the time of Domesday the church and advowson of St Cleer evidently belonged to the manor of Roscraddock, then called *Rekaradoc.* Here was a chapel of S. Winwaloe. In 1417 Sir Wm. Dawe, vicar of St Cleer, had licence to celebrate by means of a chaplain in the chapel of *S. Wynwalo* at *Craddock* in his parish. In 1421 Stephen Durnford and Radegunda his wife had licence for their chapels at Rescraddok in St Clare and Langonnet in St Vepe. In 1424, the *Capella Sancti Wynwolloci in parochia Sci Clari* was licensed during the bishop's pleasure. The chapel stood on a hill to the east of Rosecraddock, which lies in a valley. It was converted into a dwelling-house after the Reformation, and is now a small farmstead known as the Chapel House. It contains a mullioned window and some old beams, but these seem to be of the seventeenth century. "I visited the place in July 1926," writes Henderson, "but failed to discover any cut stonework or other vestiges of the once important chapel of S. Winwalo. The road running past is clearly a very ancient track. S. Winwallo's chapel at St Germans was also on a main thoroughfare."

ST GERMANS. There was a chapel of our saint in the south part of the parish of St Germans, on the north side of the old highway from Plymouth to Looe, at a place called St Winnols. "The adjacent farm, now called Eglaroose, was anciently called *Eglos-Rose, i.e.*, 'The Church on the Promontory,' showing that in Celtic times S. Winwaloe's Chapel was an independent church."[101] Field No. 3103 on this farm is called "Chapel Park." On 14

[101] C. G. Henderson. *Records of the Church and Priory of St Germans* (1929).

November 1448 Bishop Lacy granted an indulgence of forty days to all penitents visiting the chapel of *S. Wynnolous* or contributing towards its upkeep. The survey of the manor made in 1580 describes "The scyte of one Chappell latelie called ( ) cont. in length forty foot and in breadth xviij foote with an out yle [? transept] on the north side, the same being well walled with good stone and a faire roofe partely covered with slate, the residewe not covered and like shortly to decaye except yt be repaired, wch. chapel [lies] in a small pightell of good pasture environed with a stone wall wherein are trees . . . lienge north on the way to Plymouth." All traces of it have now disappeared.

PORTLEMOUTH. The church of Portlemouth, at the mouth of the River Salcombe in the extreme south of Devon, is dedicated to S. Winwaloe. From its position it may well have been founded in the Age of the Saints and connected with Breton monasteries. In Bishop Brantyngham's Register, 18 October 1372, it is *Ecclesia Sancti Wonewalai de Portelmouth*. In the inquisition held the same year it is *Sancti Wynwolay*. The name is also spelt *Onolaus*. The Rector, the Revd. C. Avery, writes "there is a local tradition that the saint used a bell to attract fishes from the sea." This "tradition," if genuine, must have come from Montreuil, but it may in reality be a modern one, due to some learned person who had read Husenbeth's *Emblems of Saints*, as there is a rival tradition that the saint was a converted Dane. There is a figure of the patron saint on one of the panels of the ancient rood-screen, which is described in Bond and Camm's *Roodscreens and Roodlofts*, vol. ii (1909), p. 344. On p. 243 is a drawing of the figure of "S. Onolaus" in its present state (there has been much "restoration" here); he is carrying a church, and has no bell or mitre.

SAINT MELANIUS or MELAINE*

PATRON OF MULLION AND ST MELLION

MELANIUS, bishop of Rennes, the patron saint of this parish, lived at the same time as S. Remigius, bishop of Rheims, and shared, it seems, in his influence over the mind of Clovis, king of the Franks. Melaine was born near Redon in Brittany, at a place called Plaz, in the parish of Brain, in the latter half of the fifth century. A local legend tells of his piety as a child. One day, while guarding his parents' flocks, he went without permission to pray at a neighbouring oratory, and remained there several hours. On his return he was punished by his mother, who put him over her knee and chastised him soundly with a birch made of broom. Since then, broom has never grown in the parish of Brain, though it is found in abundance in the surrounding parishes![1]

The young Melaine became a monk, and, later, was made abbot of his monastery. The bishop of Rennes at this period was S. Amand. Feeling that his end was near, in obedience to a supernatural revelation, he sent for Melaine. As the young

* From a sermon preached at Mullion on 15 November 1925. It was printed as no. 7 of the Cornish Saints Series (3rd edn., 1935).

[1] The story is found in a slightly different form in Sebillot's *Petite Legende dorée de la Haute Bretagne*, a very interesting and valuable collection of Breton folk-lore: "At Avessac near Redon men say that S. Melaine as a child loved to go to school at Rennes, greatly to the chagrin of his mother, who would much rather have had him become a labourer than a scholar. She often reproached him with caring so little about farm life and neglecting the cultivation of their little property. Now one day, when our saint had left his flock to go to school at Rennes, though his mother had forbidden him to do so, and the city was a long way from the little cottage ar Brain, suddenly in the middle of the lesson he heard his mother calling him, 'Melaine! Melaine!' He told his master at once that his mother was calling him, but his master thought he was mad and refused to believe him, saying that at such a distance his parent's voice could not possibly be heard. But the saint insisted, and made his teacher place his right hand in his own hand and his left foot on his own left foot. Whereupon the teacher too heard the voice of Melaine's mother, and, convinved, allowed the child to depart. Melaine, on returning home, found his mother in a furious passion. Not content with chiding him, she went out, picked a number of sprigs of broom to make a birch-rod, and administered to him a severe chastisement. Melaine thereupon forsook his home, and at his prayer, by God's permission, no broom has ever since grown in that parish. Hence the proverb still repeated in the neighbourhood:

"D'empei que sa mere le reprint,
Genet en Brain,
Melaine a Brain,
Jamais ne vint.

"Since his mother reproved him, neither broom nor Melaine was ever seen in Brain."

monk appeared among the crowd surrounding the dying prelate, Amand called him and announced that he was to be his successor in the see of Rennes. Melaine was consequently taken from his monastery by the people, after Amand had breathed his last, and acclaimed bishop. Thus Melaine became the spiritual and temporal head of this great Roman city, the most important strategic point of the West, when Clovis began to make himself master of Gaul. He became, we are told in the oldest Life of Melaine, one of Clovis's most trusted advisers. There is nothing improbable in this. The support of the bishop of Rennes was of value to Clovis in securing the adhesion of the Gallo-Roman population of the West, while the latter naturally turned to the Franks for aid against the Saxon pirates who infested the mouth of the Loire, and the British immigrants who were pouring across the English Channel.[2] We find Melaine at the Council of Orleans in 511.

You see, then, of what interest Mullion Feast on November 9 each year is to every thoughtful and instructed person. It reminds us of the power for good which the Church of Christ has exercised in the history of the world, and it reminds us that this power has again and again been exercised through the bishops, as the natural leaders and representatives of the Church. Bishops are among the greatest figures in history. England and France were converted by bishops. Our cathedrals were built in very many cases by bishops. Many of our greatest Christian books have been written by bishops. We might note, in passing, that nearly all the great bishops of antiquity to whom we owe so much—Athanasius, Ambrose, Martin, Germanus, Augustine—were chosen by popular acclamation, or designated by their predecessors. It is since bishops have been chosen by the civil power (often as a reward for political services, or for even less worthy reasons) and imposed on dioceses which had not asked for them or wished for them, that episcopal influence has declined. The appointment of bishops by the state has been one of the principal causes of the decay of religion in England and in France. If bishops in England are to recover their proper authority and influence, a change must be made in the method of their appointment.

Melaine thus played an important part in the history of France. He also played a part in the history of another country, which, though now part of France, is no more French than

[2] Lavisse, *Histoire de France*, cited by Duine.

Wales is English—I mean Brittany. Melaine is one of the saints of Brittany, but he is not a Breton saint. The Bretons in his time had only recently begun to colonize Armorica. They never colonized Rennes, and Rennes only came under the rule of a Breton king 300 years after Melaine's death.

Melaine was brought into relations with the British immigrants who were to alter the name of the country he called *Armorica* into *Brittany*, but his relations with them were not of a very friendly nature. I am afraid he regarded them very much in the light of "undesirable aliens,"—turbulent, barbarous, and of doubtful orthodoxy. A very interesting letter has been discovered, signed by Melaine and by the bishops of Tours and Angers, and addressed to two Breton priests, Lovocat and Catihern, who, in defiance of their authority, were wandering among the Breton colonists, "from cabin to cabin," celebrating the Holy Mysteries on portable altars, accompanied by women whom they called *conhospitae*, and who actually administered the chalice during the communion of the people. Melaine calls on them to "renounce these abuses".[3]

This is all we know of Melaine's relations with the Bretons. The oldest Life speaks of his evangelistic missions to what remained of the heathen Gallo-Roman population of Armorica. By raising a dead child to life he converted pagans at Vannes. He turned his family estate at Plaz into a monastery, where he frequently retired. On one occasion a fierce soldier of Vannes, named Eusebius, irritated with the people of Comblessac and Carentoir, had them brought to his camp at Marsac, where he cut off their hands and put out their eyes. He was punished for this wickedness by an agonizing paralysis of all his limbs. Thus brought to repentance, he sent for Melaine at Plaz, and the saint came, and, after imposing on him a severe penance, healed him by anointing him with consecrated oil.

Another story from the same source represents Melaine as going to Angers to visit S. Aubin. He celebrated the Holy Mysteries in a church there, and during the service distributed the *eulogia*, a kind of *pain bénit*, to bishops present with him. One of them, named Marsus, instead of eating it, concealed it in his bosom. Looking for it later on, he was horrified to find it changed into a serpent coiled round his body. He went to

[3] The Letter to Lovocat and Catihern is printed in La Borderie's *Histoire de la Bretagne*, vol. ii, pp. 526–527.

Melaine, confessed his error, received his blessing, and straightway found the serpent had once more become a harmless piece of bread. The story is, no doubt, a bit of folk-lore, inserted by the compiler of this ancient Life with the intention of doing the saint honour.

Melaine died (somewhere between 520 and 549) at Plaz, and later legends speak of the ship carrying his corpse sailing up the river Vilaine without sails or oars to Rennes, amid the chant of hymns and litanies. A story related by a contemporary writer, Gregory of Tours, gives us some interesting details about his tomb. A lofty wooden tower had been constructed over it. One day this tower took fire and was burnt to the ground, but the people, anxious lest the relics of their patron saint should have been destroyed, were overjoyed to discover that the tomb, and even the linen veil which covered it, were quite unhurt. The great abbey of S. Melaine at Rennes, which still exists, afterwards arose on the site.

After the time of Charlemagne, the Breton chief Nominoë conquered Rennes, and it became the capital of the kingdom and, later, of the duchy, of Brittany. The French-speaking part of Brittany became the more important half of the duchy[4] and the Breton kings became French dukes, but Brittany retained its regional feeling and sense of ancient independence. Melaine became a saint of Brittany, and as such is found among the Breton saints invoked in the Litany of Saint-Vougay (about 1100). His cult extends all over the diocese of Rennes, as we should expect, but we find him honoured in that of Vannes, and westwards as far as Moelan, Plobannelec and Morlaix (where a singularly beautiful fifteenth-century church bears his name). At Plélauff, in the Côtes-du-Nord, is a chapel of S. Melaine to which dogs are taken to preserve them from hydrophobia. In the diocese of Vannes he is now patron of three parish churches—Meslan, Plumelin and Rieux (the similarity of sound has caused this, no doubt, in the case of the first two), and of chapels in the parishes of Lanvénégen and Lignol (Duhem, *Églises du Morbihan*). There are three holy wells of S. Melaine in the east of Brittany.

The Shrine of S. Sever, formerly kept in the cathedral at Rouen and now in the Musée des Antiquités in that city, contained, besides the body of S. Sever, "the arms of Saint Sulpice,

[4] We have a parallel case in our own island. The Celtic kings of Scotland conquered the English-speaking Lowlands which then became the predominant part of their kingdom.

Saint Germaine and Saint *Melaigne*".[5] Our saint appears in sixth and seventh century revisions of the Hieronymian Martyrology on January 6 and November 6: M. Calan says that his cult spread through Christendom more quickly than that of any other saint of Brittany (*Mélanges Historiques*, pp. 3ff.), S. Melaine was honoured in the north and east of France (his fame reached Burgundy and the diocese of Metz at an early date, says Duine)[6] and in England. A sacramentary belonging to an unknown church in the north of France, written in the tenth or eleventh century, has the feast of his Translation on October 11.[7] The fourteenth-century copy of the Exeter Martyrology has the words "Redonis, Brittannie minoris, sancti Melanii, episcopi et confessoris, qui post signa virtutum, jugiter intentus celo, migravit a seculo" under January 6. "Depositio sancti Melani episcopi et confessoris" is an early ninth-century addition made in France to the Martyrology of Bede.[8] Célestin Port, in his *Dictionnaire historique de Maine-et-Loire* (1878), tells us that there were two churches of S. Melaine in Anjou, one in the commune of Cholet called "Saint-Melaine-les-Sources" or "de la Treille" (formerly in the diocese of La Rochelle), the other in the commune of Segré. Both are now destroyed.

As a well-known saint of Brittany, Melaine at last actually supplanted the original patron saint of this parish: he cannot possibly ever have come to Mullion. The original patron of Mullion, who may be the same as the Breton S. Mollien or Moellien,[9] was a compatriot of the Lovocat and Catihern with whom Melaine was so little in sympathy. But both your patrons, the old and the new, are a tie between you and that most fascinating and romantic land, the land of heroism and deepest religious feeling—Brittany.

Melaine is also now, and since the thirteenth century at any rate, the patron of S. Mellion in East Cornwall, of which, according to Loth, S. Mellon was the original patron. I can find no authority for the latter assertion. In the Taxation of Pope Nicholas IV (1288-1291) St Mellion is called *Ecclesia Sancti Mellani*, and assessed at £4. S. Mellon is a saint honoured both in

[5] Farcy, *Histoire de la paroisse Saint-Sever de Rouen* (1933), pp. 28-29. S. Melain or Melaine is patron of the chapel of the castle at Auzebosc (Seine Inf.), 15 kil. from Héricourt.

[6] *Inventaire liturgique de l'hagiographie bretonne*, 1922, pp. 26 and 34.

[7] "Et translatio corporis sancti Melani episcopi et confessoris" (Duine, *loc. cit.*)

[8] Dom Quentin, *Les Martyrologes historiques*, p. 25.

[9] Loth, *Noms des saints bretons*, p. 92.

H

Brittany (at Melon and at a chapel in the parish of Tréogat, between Pont l'Abbé and Audierne, in Finistère) and in Normandy.[10] There is a late and untrustworthy Life of this saint, according to which he was born at Cardiff, and became bishop of Rouen. He was believed to have founded the church of S. Lô in Rouen, and pilgrims visited the church in great numbers on his day. At Rouen, and in the printed Breviary of the diocese of Léon in Brittany (1516), his feast is October 22. In the Rouen Breviary of 1728 is a hymn beginning:

> Quantis Rotomagus sub tenebris jacet,
> Cum Christum resonans, vox sacra Numinis,
> Nos Mellonus, aperto
> Veri lumine, recreat!

There was no church dedicated to him in Rouen, but there was a collegiate church of S. Melon at Pontoise (where was also a church dedicated to another Celtic saint—S. Maclou), and the parish of Saint-Denis-sur-Héricourt, north of Yvetot in the Pays de Caux, was "vulgairement appelée Saint-Melon" in the eighteenth century (Féron, *Notes . . . sur la réception de la Bulle Unigenitus dans le diocèse de Rouen*, pp. 52, 65, 70). Near Héricourt, on the road between Yvetot and Cany, is a holy well, called "Le petit Saint-Mellon," where the saint is said to have been baptized! It was, up to fifty years ago, M. Féron tells me, the object of a popular pilgrimage, especially on Whit Monday. The only parish church in the diocese of Rouen dedicated to S. Mellon, he writes, is that of Thiédeville, between Rouen and Dieppe, north-west of Totes.[11] Roman antiquities abound in the neighbourhood, which was "a great centre of population under the later emperors" (Cochet). It is remarkable that the twelfth-century Exeter Martyrology commemorated S. Mellon on June 6, coupling him with the Celtic S. Branwalader—"beatorum confessorum et episcoporum Branwaladri et mellonis." Near Newport in Monmouthshire is a parish of *St Mellons* or *St Mellans*, where S. Melanus is patron.

There is a holy well at St Mellion in Cornwall. The parish

[10] *cf.* Duine, *Mémento*, No. 171, *Invent. Lit.*, p. 175.

[11] M. Féron writes to me that "according to some authorities the dedication of the church of Thiédeville is to S. Nicaise. S. Mellon shared with S. Nicaise, S. Romain, S. Ouen, S. Ansbert and S. Victrice in the patronage of the confraternity of the eight minor canons of Rouen cathedral."

contained in 1448, it is interesting to note, a chapel of S. Elidius, Bishop, a Celtic saint honoured in West Cornwall and the Isles of Scilly.

§

The ancient Life of Melaine, referred to in this sketch, is a document "the historical residuum of which is very slender. It exists in three versions, of which the oldest is not earlier than the eleventh century, in the opinion of Krusch, Molinier and Duchesne." (Duine, *Mémento*, No. 13.) The letter to Lovocat and Catihern, which is of undoubted authenticity and of the very first importance (it was discovered by Mgr Duchesne) was written between 515 and 520. The reference to his tomb at Rennes by Gregory of Tours (died 594) is also of interest and importance as practically contemporary evidence. The relics and miracles of Melaine are referred to in a letter of Gervais, archbishop of Rheims (1055—1067) to Even, abbot of Saint-Melaine. Albert Le Grand (17th century) of course fills his story of the saint with his own picturesque fancies and inserts the most amazing anachronisms.

C. G. Henderson writes "Melian appears to have been the way both places, St Mellion and Mullion, were pronounced in the middle ages. Mullion occurs as *Eglosmeylyon juxta Lanfrouder* in 1343. The personal name Melyan occurs in numerous place-names in Cornwall—*Trevelyan* in St Veep, *Trevellan* (formerly Trevelien) in Luxulyan, *Rosemullion* (Rosemelyan) in Mawnan and Luxulyan. *Lamellyn* is a common Cornish place-name, but it is almost invariably a corruption of Nans-melyn = the mill valley (melin = mill). Where however the name is Lamellion it is more probable that the personal name Melan or Melion is intended. At Lemellyn or Lamellion in Lanteglos by Fowey (always written *Lamelyon* in the middle ages) is the site of the chapel or hermitage of S. Wyllow, who (according to the garbled version of his legend as given by William of Worcester in 1478) was beheaded here 'by Melyn ys kynrede' (*i.e.*, the kinsfolk of Melyn). In Liskeard is a place called Lamellion where was a chapel of the B.V.M. in 1442 (Lamelen) but this name may be Nans-melyn, the mill valley."

A moor on the Cury boundary of the parish, some way from the churchtown, is called *St Maloes* Moor in 1840, but I cannot discover any older authority for the name. I do not think Porthmellin has any more significance than its English translation "Mullion cove."

I need hardly point out that the saints mentioned by the late Revd. E. G. Harvey, formerly vicar of Mullion, in his description of the parish, as possible patrons of Mullion, have no more claim to the title than "the plant Mullen." "S. Mellonus is called S. Malo by Ussher; and Dr Oliver decides that Mellonus, Malo and Meen are identical, and seeing that we have S. Malo's moor in the parish to this day, I would rather suppose that S. Malo, a Briton by birth, gave the name to this parish than go out of my way to seek, as some have done, in the Persian language, for a word resembling 'Mullyon' and meaning 'smooth,' particularly as there is nothing smooth about us either by sea or on land—than trace it to the plant 'Mullen' which really grows in much greater abundance in the neighbouring parishes than with us, or, than place myself under the patronage of S. Melanie" (p. 2). "S. Malo, it would appear, was a man of many aliases—as Mellonus or Melanus, Melanius, Melan, Melonius Britannus, Mellion, Maclovius, Maclou, Machutus, Mahut, Menvennus, Mawes and Meen—perhaps some others also" (p. 22). He would indeed be a man of many aliases if these were all his names, but as a matter of fact they are the names of at least six different persons. SS. Melon, Melaine, Maclovius (Malo), Machutus (a saint of the city of Saintes in Saintonge, mistakenly, though at a very early period, identified with Maclovius of Aleth), Mewan and Maudez (Mawes) are all confused here. Mr Harvey admits that the parish feast is on November 6, the feast of S. Melaine at Rennes, not on November 15, the feast of S. Machutus (Malo), and it is quite certain that S. Melaine of Rennes has been the patron saint of Mullion since the early middle ages. No one at the present day pays any attention to Dr Oliver's "decision" that "Mellonus, Malo and Meen are identical," which they certainly are not.

The editorial note inserted underneath the view of the rood-screen in Mullion church in *The English Churchman's Kalendar* for 1928 has, I fear, given widespread currency to a most deplorable blunder made by Sabine Baring-Gould about the dedication of Mullion church. It states that "Celtic scholars do not now attribute its foundation to a visit from St Melanius, Bishop of Rennes in the sixth century, but to St Melyan, Prince of Cornwall, who was put to death about 524."

I have explained the error made by Baring-Gould, in my *Saint Melor* (no. 43 in the Cornish Saints Series). The father of the little martyr prince Melor was Meliavus, prince of *Armorican* Cornwall. Both father and son were murdered by Rivoldus, the brother of Meliavus. Meliavus was regarded as a martyr as well as his son, and is venerated in Brittany as the patron of Plou-Miliau and Gui-Miliau. In some manuscripts of the Life of S. Melor his father's name was by mistake written Melianus instead of Meliavus. Baring-Gould fell into the snare, and unblushingly made Meliavus into an imaginary Melyan, prince of *our own* Cornwall and patron of Mullion and St Mellion! Meliavus is a purely Armorican (Breton) saint, his cult is unknown on this side of the Channel; and the patron of Mullion church was, in all probability, as I have stated, originally a Celtic monk and missionary who worked both in Cornwall and Brittany. When the story of his life was at last forgotten, the famous Gallo-Roman bishop of Rennes, Melanius, whose name resembled his, took his place as patron of Mullion and St Mellion.

In Brittany there is a story that in the commune of Avessac there is a family almost every member of which has seven or eight fingers on each hand. Local tradition claims that this monstrosity is a punishment inflicted at Melaine's prayer when one day he saw someone of this family pulling out the hairs of his horse's tail.

At Pléchatel, on the Vilaine between Rennes and Redon, may be seen the ruins of a chapel of S. Melaine on the banks of a brook. Under the walls of the chancel, beneath the site of the altar, rises the holy well of S. Melaine. The country people make a pilgrimage to this place in time of drought to ask for rain. They bring a pig's trotters as an offering, and one of the pilgrims sprinkles with water from the fountain a piece of wood, the remains of a statue of the saint, saying:

Saint Melaine, mon bon Saint Melaine,
Arrose nous, comme je t'arrose.

"Saint Melaine, my good Saint Melaine,
Water us as I water thee."

These curious scraps of folk-lore show how strong is the hold S. Melaine still has on the imagination of the people of the country districts south of Rennes.

A sequence hymn in honour of S. Melaine (first found in the Missal of Aemar Hennequin, bishop of Rennes, 1588) is sung in the diocese of Rennes, beginning:

Nostri patris et pastoris
Melanii Confessoris
Dignas laudes cordis, oris,
    Nostra pangat concio . . .

Vitam duxit monachalem,
Nactus sedem cathedralem:
Gerens curam pastoralem,
    Vita, verbo docuit.

Hunc vocavit rex Francorum,
Per quem status clericorum
Restauratur: idolorum
    Evanescit vanitas . . .

Mr Athelstan Riley has made a translation of this sequence and it is sung to a French plainsong melody as an office hymn in Mullion church at the Feast. One verse,

See the saints and prelates hurrying
To our good S. Melaine's burying,
    By divine monition sent![12]

refers to the following legend: "The news of Melaine's death spread rapidly, and soon brought to Plaz the bishops of the neighbouring dioceses, who all cherished a strong affection for him—S. Aubin (Albinus) of Angers, S. Lô (Lauton) of Coutances, Victurius of Le Mans, and a great crowd of priests, among them his favourite disciple, Marsus. After the solemn watching of the body and the celebration of the funeral rites by the bishops and clergy at Plaz, the body of the pious pontiff was placed in a barge, in which the three bishops and Marsus took their places. Other vessels followed, full of people, with many priests and the monks of Plaz, chanting psalms and litanies. The cortege proceeded

[12] Sancti plures et prelati
Sunt a Deo ad beati
Exequias destinati,
    Praestantes obsequia.

Ad urbem quam ante rexit
Christo duce, navis vexit,
Clarum corpus et reflexit
    Cursum Vicenonia.

up the river to Rennes, and landed at what is now the Escalier du Cartage, at the bottom of the rue de Rohan. Close by, forming part of the old Gallo-Roman wall of the city, stood a tower in which twelve prisoners were awaiting execution. Hearing the sound of the chanting, the unhappy captives implored the saint to intercede for them. Suddenly a roar was heard, the wall of the tower gaped wide from top to bottom, the prisoners leaped through the breach and joined the funeral procession of their liberator" (La Borderie.)

The prayers of S. Melaine are invoked especially in time of public calamities.

At Rennes the name is pronounced *M'laine*, and sometimes *Blaine*.

SAINT RUMON*

Patron of the Ruans

JOHN Leland, "the King's Antiquary," to whom students of local history are under so great a debt for his survey of Cornwall (and other counties), compiled towards the end of the reign of King Henry VIII (he came to Cornwall in 1538), made in his notebooks a few brief extracts from the Lives of two Cornish saints which he had seen in the course of his travels, the Life of S. Nectan and the Life of S. Rumon, who were the patrons of two of the most important abbeys in the west of England in the middle ages—Hartland and Tavistock. These Lives had since disappeared, and it was feared that they were lost for ever, but they were both found in a most valuable fourteenth-century collection of Lives of English saints, forming MS. M.n.57 in the Ducal Library of Gotha (the discovery was made by Mr Francis Wormald, of the British Museum, in 1937).

I have translated the *Vita Nectani* of the Gotha MS. [see Cornish Saints Series, no. 45] and I now give a translation of the *Vita Rumonis* from the same manuscript, and discuss some of the problems it presents.

The newly discovered Life of S. Rumon turns out to be (as scholars had already surmised from Leland's extracts from it[1]) mainly an adaptation of the Breton *Vita Ronani*, the name *Ronanus* being altered throughout to *Rumonus*,[2] and a postscript added, describing the translation of S. Rumon's body to Tavistock. It will therefore be necessary first to examine the Breton traditions about *S. Ronan*, and also to marshall the few scraps of information about *S. Rumon* afforded us by the study of place-names in Devon and Cornwall and in Brittany, and by entries in kalendars

* Cornish Saints Series, no. 42 (1939).

1 "Rumonus genere fuit Scottus Hibernensis. Nemea sylva in Cornubia plenissima olim ferarum, S. Rumonus faciebat sibi oratorium in sylva Nemaea . . . . Falemutha. Ordulphus, dux Cornubiae, transtulit ossa Rumoni Tavistochium" (*De rebus Britannicis Collectanea*, iv. pp. 152-3). The extract comes at the end of a short list of books apparently in the library of Tavistock Abbey, and headed *Tavestoke*. The list ends "S. Rumonus sepultus apud Tavestoke." Then follows the extract *Ex vita Rumoni*. (The list follows a list of books at Plympton Priory, and is followed (after the extract from S. Rumon's Life) by a list of books at Hartland Abbey.)

2 The grammatical discrepancy between the form of the saint's name in the title of the *Vita* and that uniformly adopted in the text will be referred to later.

and other hagiographical documents on this side of the Channel, in order to see what justification, if any, can be found for our author's identification of S. Rumon with S. Ronan.

Saint Ronan is well known to everyone who has visited Lower Brittany through the magnificent church dedicated to him at Locronan, near Quimper, containing his bell and beautifully carved fifteenth-century "tomb", and scenes from his Life painted on the pulpit; and through the famous Pardon, the chief of all the Breton Pardons, called the Grande Troménie of Locronan, which is held there every sixth year.[3] It is for this reason, and not for anything certainly true that we know about his place in the history of Brittany, that Canon Calvez has given a chapter on S. Ronan in his charmingly illustrated little book *Les grands saints bretons* (Grenoble, 1936). S. Ronan was also, before the Revolution, patron of one of the parishes of the city of Quimper, called Saint-Ronan de la Rue Obscure,[4] and of a chapel and holy well at Plozévet, and a chapel and *Penity* at Briec in the same diocese. Outside Cornouaille, he has a considerable cult in the north of Brittany. He is patron of the little town of Saint-Renan in Léon, and of the church on the island of Molène between Ushant and the mainland; and of Laurenan (=Lok Renan; in the fifteenth-century it was written *Lauregnan*—there is a very ancient cross here, and some fields called *Menehy*, and a holy well) and of Hillion in the diocese of Saint-Brieuc. S. Ronan was formerly patron of three chapels in the diocese of Tréguier (*Locrenan* in Plestin, *Saint-Renan* in Ploeuc, and *Saint-Drenean* in Minihy Tréguier), and in this way has given his name to the celebrated critic Ernest Renan, who was, as everyone knows, a native of Tréguier.

S. Ronan has a liturgical cult in at any rate three out of the four Breton dioceses which contain churches or chapels dedicated in his honour. His name is found, on June 1, in the kalendars of Cornouaille (1642, 1701, 1789), Léon (*Ronani, episcopi*, 1516) and Tréguier (15th cent.), but not in those of Saint-Brieuc; and in the kalendar of the Missal of Breventec (13th cent.). He is invoked in the Litany of Limoges (11th cent.), where he is placed in a group of saints honoured in the bishoprics of Saint-Brieuc, Tréguier

[3] The procession of the Grande Troménie follows a course 13 kilometres in length. It has been described by the Duke of Argyll in *A Breton Pilgrimage*, and by Anatole le Braz in *Au Pays des Pardons*. The Petite Troménie, held every year, is much shorter.

[4] Now the chapel of N.D. des Carmes.

and Léon.[5] In the statutes of the synod of the diocese of Cornouaille in 1536 his feast was a *fête chomée*, on which no work might be done.

S. Ronan has a large number of dedications in Brittany, many of which can have had no connection with the later priory of Locronan in Cornouaille. I think then that we can unhesitatingly dismiss the contention of R. Latouche (*Mélanges d'histoire de Cornouaille*, Paris, 1911, p. 95) that "the Armorican S. Ronan never existed, and his legend is a toponymic legend suggested by the name *Locronan*." Latouche does not offer any other explanation of the name, and Breton place-names beginning with *Loc* almost invariably contain the name of a saint whose *locus* was situated in the place in question. *Ronan* is the name of a saint—it is the Irish form of the name *Romanus* (the Martyrology of Donegal gives twelve different saints called Ronan), as *Rumon* is the British form. The fact that Ronan is an *Irish* form in a British land is a difficulty which will be discussed later, together with the question of the date, authorship and trustworthiness of his legend.

Saint Rumon has been the patron from a very early period (if not from the beginning) of the great abbey of Tavistock in Devon. He is the patron, too, of the church of Romansleigh in that county, where there is also a holy well called after him. In Cornwall he is the patron of three parishes: Ruan Lanihorne on the Fal, and Ruan Major and Ruan Minor near the Lizard; and was the patron of the chapel of the town of Redruth, destroyed in the eighteenth century.[6] The abbey of Glastonbury possessed in the fourteenth century "a bone of Saint Rumon." He is also the original patron of the church of the town of Audierne in Armorican Cornwall, and of Saint-Jean-Trolimon a little to the south.[7] At Audierne he has been replaced by a modern saint

[5] Duine, *Inventaire liturgique*, pp. 60, 75, 206, 214, 229. For the cult of S. Ronan, see Dr Dujardin, *Saint Ronan* (Brest, 1935). English readers will be familiar with the name Ronan through Sir Walter Scott's novel *St. Ronan's Well* (The scene is laid at the medicinal spring at Innerleithen on the Tweed).

[6] "in capella Sancti Rumani [*sic*] in villa sive hameletta de Redruth" (Bp. Stafford's Register, 1400 and 1405). Polruan at the mouth of the Fowey may not have anything to do with S. Rumon. In an early 13th cent. deed it is spelt *Porruwan* (*Por* = Porth). In 1331 it was *Polrewan*. Mr Henderson thought it might possibly mean "The Roman Port." At Indian Queens in the parish of St Columb Major is a longstone with an inscription, which Dr Borlase in 1750 read as RUANI HIC JACET. But Professor Macalister reads the name CRVARIG (*Arch. Camb.*, Dec. 1929, p. 183).

[7] "The church of Saint Rumon of Audierne" is mentioned in 1633. "Trolimon" was formerly *Treff Rumon* (Loth, *Noms*, p. 111). "Ruan represents *Ruvon* in Cornish. . . . One of the sons of the celebrated Cunedda, *Rumaun*, has given his name to *Rhufoniog* in Wales" (ib.).

whose name sounded rather like his—S. Raymond Nonnatus, but Canon Pérennès, of Quimper, tells me that the fishermen there still invoke "Saint Rumon."

The chief settlement of S. Rumon in Cornwall was no doubt, as his *Vita* says, at Ruan Lanihorne. The great estuaries were the earliest centres of civilization in the West Country. By the Fal ships could penetrate into the heart of Cornwall, and monks in monasteries built close to its deep and tranquil harbours could communicate with Brittany in a few hours, when the wind was favourable. A very ancient road, as we shall see, comes down to the Fal not far from Ruan church. But unfortunately all records of the history of this interesting place in the days before the Norman Conquest have perished, and for this period we have nothing to guide us but the evidence of place-names.

The parish is usually referred to in medieval documents by its second name (*Ecclesia de Larihorn*, 1283 and 1308, *Laryhorn* 1328, *Lanryhoern* 1329, *Lanihorne* 1339, *Larihorne* 1340, *Laryhorne* 1351, *Lanyhorne* 1376). Professor Loth pointed out that an anchorite at the abbey of Saint-Gildas-en-Rhuys in Brittany in the early middle ages, venerated there as a martyr, was called *Ehoarn*. But the eponym of Lanyhorne, as Mr Henderson shows, cannot have borne this name, since the early forms all contain an *R* at the beginning of the second half of the name. He suggested that *Laryhorn* might mean *Lan-Ruan*. But the persistence of the letter *r* before the *n* or *ne* seems to forbid this. The name of the eponym seems to be *Ryhorn*. Usually in Cornwall, where the name of a parish begins with *Lan*, or has (as often happens) an alternative name beginning *Lan*, the parish church is not dedicated to the eponym of the Lan. We have an example close by at St Just (Lansioch), and other examples are Crantock, Fowey, Lelant, Madron and Gulval. Ruan Lanihorne is almost unique in Cornwall in having the two saints' names now permanently combined.

The church of Lanihorne is dedicated to S. Rumon, and the survival of the vernacular form *Ruan* here seems a proof of the vigour of his cult. He had a holy well in the adjoining parish of Veryan, for a map of Tregongan in the parish in the year 1694 shows a field below the farmhouse, and close to the Ruan border, which it calls *Park-Venton-Ruan*. A stream rises here which flows down to Ruan Creek.

On the site of the present church of Ruan Lanihorne there

must once have been a Celtic oratory surrounded by monastic cells. We cannot of course take seriously the story of the *Vita Rumonis* that the saint's body was brought there from Brittany in the tenth century. Probably S. Rumon was buried at Lanihorne, and his body remained there till its removal by Ordulph. In the transept of the present church is a "demi-effigy in Purbeck stone of an ecclesiastic within a cusped arch of late thirteenth-century date," discovered during the restoration of 1866. It was declared by some to be the shrine of S. Rumon, but J. Charles Cox says it is "only part of a sepulchral stone to some distinguished ecclesiastic." This may be so, but it is quite likely that there was a shrine of S. Rumon in the church down to the Reformation. Many Cornish churches possessed shrines containing the bodies of their patron saints. Ordulph may have left part of the relics at Ruan. The tomb of S. Neot still exists on the north side of the chancel of his church in Cornwall, in spite of the carrying off of at any rate part of the body to Huntingdonshire in the eleventh century. The saint was certainly duly honoured at Ruan down to the end of the middle ages. In 1525 we find Marion, relict of Stephen Lelley, leaving in her will a cow to the Store of Saint Rumonus, and appointing Reginald Tregian, rector of Lanyhorne, one of her executors.

The Lizard peninsula has a close connection with S. Rumon. Two parish churches there are dedicated to him, while a chapel, holy well and cross in Grade also bear his name.

Ruan Major is referred to in a deed of 1325 as *Merther*[8] while the bridge near the church, now called Ponsa-medda, is therein called *Pons-merther* (it was still called Pons-an-Merther in 1757). It is called *Ecclesia Sancti Rumoni de Withientone* in 1207, because, unlike the other four Lizard churches, it did not lie within the great fief that bore the various names of Lantyan, Rosewick, Trethevas or Lucyes, but in the royal manor of Winnianton.

The little parish of Ruan Minor lay within the manor of Trethevas, to which the advowson was appended. In 1277 it is called *Ecclesia de Sancto Rumono Parvo in Manerio de Tredevos;*

[8] The bounds of the manor of Tredeves pass by "the stone called Hyrven, and thence by the sanctuary [glebe] of Merther to the bridge of Merther . . . . to the moor of John Marsily of Saint Rumon." The word *merther* is of course derived from *martyrion*, meaning originally a chapel in honour of a martyr: it came to mean a chapel in honour of any saint, *not* necessarily a martyr.

Ecclesia Sancti Rumoni Parvi 1313, *Ruan Minor in Morrep* 1442, *St Rumon in Terra Arida* 1460.

Tradition and place-names all bear witness to a personal connection between S. Rumon and the picturesque valley between Grade and Ruan Minor. Here is an estate that has long been known as "St Ruan", and on this is a field called Park Chapel (Nos. 558 and 552), while the next field is called Park Venton, from a spring which is said to be a holy well. It is by the side of the footpath from "St Ruan" to Ruan Minor church and is just inside that parish. The Chapel Close however is in Grade, across the brook. The field to the north, also in Grade, is called Park an Grouse. In the centre stands a rude pillar of hornblende, locally called "S. Ruan's Cross." It is 3 feet high and of the roughest description: it has no sign of carving and the back is unhewn (see Langdon, *Old Cornish Crosses*, p. 91). In the large common field or "praze" of the hamlet of Bruggan, ¼ mile north-east of Grade church, is the spring called "Grade Well" or "S. Ruan's Well," It is covered by a simple little rectangular building of serpentine, except the arched entrance (62 ins. high and 29 ins. wide), which is of granite. The water is still used for baptisms at Grade.

The feast of the Translation of S. Rumon is entered in the Exeter Martyrology on January 5, and that of the death on August 30, both as being observed at Tavistock.[9] The list of relics at Glastonbury gives the very interesting statement that the saint was "the brother of S. Tidwal."[10] His name is in the kalendar of the book of hours of Launceston Priory discovered by Mr Francis Wormald at Little Malvern Court, on August 30 (*S. Rumoni*). Mr Wormald suggests that "some arrangement was made between the priory of Launceston and abbey of Tavistock whereby each house honoured the other's patron. . . . Such arrangements are known in the middle ages."[11]

Let us now turn to the Gotha Life of S. Rumon, of which the following is an English translation.

[9] "*Nonis Januarij* . . . Ipso die in Anglia, Tavistochie monasterio translacio sancti Rumonis confessoris . . . . iij Kal. Septembris . . . . Eodem die, sancti Rumoni episcopi et confessoris, apud monasterium Tauistochie in diocesi Exoniensi quiescentis."

[10] "A bone of S. Rumon, brother of S. Tidwal" (*Chronica sive Historia de rebus glastoniensibus*, ed. Th. Hearne, Oxonie, 1726, p. 450). Glastonbury had connection with the Lizard district.

[11] *Journal of Theological Studies*, Jan., 1938, pp. 8, 18, 19.

INCIPIT VITA SANCTI RUMONIS

VIJ KALENDAS JULIJ

The blessed Rumonus, who is also called Ronanus by the Irish, whose body, with the sole exception of the head, now rests in Devon, at Tavistock, near Cornwall,[12] was born in Ireland and was a Scot by race. There [*i.e.*, in Ireland], by reason of his sanctity and his knowledge of Holy Scripture, he was finally raised to the episcopate. Afterwards he left his native country, crossed the ocean and came to Lesser Britain, and landed on the coasts of Léon, and from thence he came to Cornouaille, which by the Bretons is called Cornuguallia. For Lesser Britain is divided into three portions each having its own count, namely Cornouaille, Rennes and Vannes. These three counts, namely the Count of Cornouaille, the Count of Rennes and the Count of Vannes, had one king over them, called Grallon, who was monarch over the whole Breton people. So Rumon or Ronan, coming to Cornouaille, which is the western portion of Lesser Britain, built there an oratory for himself near the great wood called the Nemean wood.[13]

Now there lived near the same oratory a certain very religious peasant, who heard of his sanctity and the wonderful works which God wrought for him, and recognized the truth of the holy doctrine which he taught, and used to visit the holy man almost daily, and loved him, and used to remain with him as long as his affairs permitted him to do so. Grallon also, the king of the Bretons, a most holy man, hearing of his sanctity, gladly visited him, and laid up in his heart the counsels that he gave him, and practised the same. The neighbours also used to flock to hear him, and were edified by his preaching. But the wife of the aforesaid peasant, who was called Keban, grew jealous and displeased that her husband left her alone, and spent too much of his time with the holy man, and she went to the latter and reviled him, saying that it was by his fault she had lost her husband, who was now more a monk than a husband. But the holy man ever replied gently and patiently to all her abuse, and endeavoured, so far as he could, to pacify her.

In the aforesaid wood there lurked wolves and many other ravenous beasts, which used by night (and even by day) to devour the flocks of those who lived in the neighbourhood. Now one day the holy man beheld a wolf passing before the door of his oratory, carrying a sheep in its mouth and making for the wood. He bade it drop the sheep, and it did so immediately. And the holy man saw that the sheep was returned to its owner. This he did more than once, and often, by his word alone, he delivered the neighbour's sheep and cattle from beasts of prey. For these and other charitable deeds all the people of that district respected the holy man, who protected them and their flocks; they constantly visited him, and blessed him and gave him thanks for all he did for them.

But the Devil, envying his good works, and the love which the people of

[12] *In Deuonia apud Tauestochiam, prope Cornubiam.* In this Life the two Cornwalls, the insular and the Armorican, are alike called *Cornubia.* In my translation I have called them *Cornwall* and *Cornouaille* respectively, to avoid confusion.

[13] The forest of Névet, the remains of which still exist in the commune of Plogonnec. It is the "silva que vocatur Nemet" of the *Cartula Sancti Ronani* (dated 1031) in the Cartulary of Quimperlé (pp. 138—145).

the place had for him, stirred up the aforesaid Keban, the wife of the aforesaid peasant, to be an adversary of the holy man, because her husband spent more time with him than she liked. So the wicked woman invented a malicious falsehood against him, saying that he used every month, at the new moon, to change himself into a wolf and devour the neighbour's sheep and cattle. And she spread this evil report concerning him everywhere throughout the whole province, among all the people and even in the ears of the king. And, to give colour to the accusation, she said that he had eaten her only daughter, who was five years old, and she hid the child away in a chest, so that none should see her, intending to feed her secretly with bread and milk. But, by the just judgement of God, the first morsel of bread the child swallowed choked her, and she died as a punishment of her mother's wickedness. Now the king, when he heard the woman's lying story, sent for the holy man, not for that he himself believed what she said, but in order that his sanctity, impugned by her accusations, might thereby be the more widely known. So the holy man came to the king's court, and sat down on a stone in front of the gate, tired with his journey, for he was an old man.

Then the king, by the advice of his counsellors, whose minds had begun to waver owing to the woman's pertinacity in complaining of her daughter's death, set two fierce dogs he kept, which were used to drive off other animals, and to keep away strangers and mind cattle, to attack the holy man. But when they flew upon him, he raised his hand and made the sign of the cross, and immediately they lay down at his feet, and became perfectly tame and gentle. When the king and his counsellors saw this, they marvelled, and came to the holy man, asking pardon for what they had done, proclaiming his holiness and innocence. The woman Keban however persisted in her malice, and springing into the midst, reviled the holy man, asserting loudly that he had eaten her daughter. But he, taught by the Holy Ghost, told them all what the aforesaid woman had done to her daughter, and also that the girl was lying dead in the chest, choked by the morsel of bread. Then the king sent in haste to the woman's house, and found everything as the holy man had said. When this was known, the people wished to stone Keban, but the holy man delivered her out of their hands. So Keban gave glory to God, and fell penitently at the holy man's feet, weeping and asking for forgiveness, and desiring him that he would raise her daughter to life. And he prayed to God that this might be, and restored the girl alive to her mother, and thus the holy man's sanctity was acknowledged and glorified by all.

After this, the aforesaid Keban was again stirred up by Satan against the holy man, on account of her husband spending so much time with him, as we have said already. So in order to turn her husband's friendship into hostility, she told him, and also asserted publicly, that the holy man *cum ea concumbere voluit*. And he, perceiving that the woman's hatred of him would never cease so long as she lived, determined to retire to some remote spot, that so at any rate her envy might abate when he was no longer there. But he cursed Keban, and she was smitten with leprosy and received the due reward of her deeds. So Saint Rumon withdrew from Cornouaille, and journeying eastwards came into the province of Rennes, and with the aid of a certain religious man, who gave him hospitality, he built for himself an oratory in the parts of Domnonia near Hilion, where he lived in great abstinence to the day of his death, his host ministering to his needs. After his decease his host came one day and found him dead, lying in an attitude of prayer; and he grieved greatly for his death, and wept, and would not be comforted. He knew moreover that he would be robbed of his body, since the three counts aforesaid, when they heard of his death, would come and carry it away to bury it with honour. Thinking over this, and wishing to have some relics of the holy man, moved with pious zeal, he cut off one of his arms and carried it home with him. But the night following he awoke from sleep and perceived that his own arm had been cut off. He saw that this had happened as a punishment for what he had done, and, repenting, he went with tears to the oratory, and asked for pardon, and placed the holy man's arm by his body, and straightway it was joined to it again. By his merits also his own arm was restored to him while he slept in the oratory, so that when he awoke he felt no harm.

Now the three counts aforesaid, namely the Count of Cornouaille, the Count of Rennes and the Count of Vannes, when they heard of the death of Saint Rumon, came straightway to his oratory. Each of them strove to have the holy body handed to him, to bury in his own province, and they took counsel and agreed to place the holy body on a wagon to be drawn by two three-year-old oxen who had never been yoked, and that whithersoever those oxen bore the holy body, to that province it should belong. But the counts could not lift the body from the ground, even with the assistance of others they asked to help them, so they took counsel and decided that the body should be delivered to that one by whom it should allow itself to be lifted. The Count of Rennes and the Count of Vannes tried and failed, but when the Count of Cornouaille, in whose province the holy man had first lived, came, in spite of his right arm being paralysed he easily lifted the body and placed it on the wagon, and he recovered the use of his arm by the merits of the holy man. Then the oxen, turning neither to the right nor to the left, without any to guide them, with one accord began to draw the wagon into Cornouaille. And when they had come to a certain valley, which is called in the vernacular Tnoubalan, the oxen stood still and could proceed no further. The valley is distant one mile from the oratory which the holy man formerly built for himself by the Nemean wood. The consul, seeing this and wondering, inspired by the Holy Ghost, gave the whole of that land, from the aforesaid valley to the oratory and round about, to Saint Rumon in perpetuity. Then the oxen immediately proceed to the oratory with the body; the sacred body is taken down from the wagon and carried with rejoicing into the oratory, and there honourably buried. It rested there for a long time, conferring many benefits on those who prayed there.

But afterwards, when many years had elapsed, the whole of Brittany was depopulated by pirates. Then the people (*gens*), leaving their own habitation, was dispersed through divers parts of the world, carrying with them the body of the blessed Rumon and of Saint Winwaloe the Abbot who became everywhere famous through the miracles he worked.[14] At last, however, the head of the blessed Rumon was first restored to Cornouaille, and later the rest of his members which the people had carried away with them, as we have said, were

[14] A comparison with the corresponding passage in the *Vita Ronani* shows that the reference is to the miracles said to have been worked by S. Winwaloe in his lifetime, as mentioned in his *Vita*.

brought back into Cornouaille, to the town called Confluencia [Quimper], and honourably placed in the basilica of the glorious pontiff Saint Courentin, amid a great concourse of clergy and people. Now while the sacred body was reposing in this basilica, by his merits a man dumb from birth, thinking on the relics of Saint Rumon and praying earnestly to him, received the power of speech and cried distinctly three times, "Rumon."

At another time also a certain madman, with his hands tied behind his back, was brought to the body of the blessed Rumon, and the night following was placed near the shrine containing the relics of the holy man. Next day he was entirely cured. And many others also have been cured there by the merits of Saint Rumon.

At another time also a certain building in the aforesaid Confluencia was set on fire, and the flames blazed so fiercely that it was thought the whole city would be burned down. After vain endeavours to extinguish the fire by water and other means, the body of the holy Rumon was carried thither by the clergy. Then all began to cry, "Saint Ruman, help thy servants," and immediately the conflagration lost its power, sank down and was extinguished.

Afterwards however the aforesaid relics of Saint Rumon were transferred from Confluencia into the Cornwall of Greater Britain, and placed in the church of the *villa* which is called Lanrihorn. And there they remained in a shrine (*feretrum*) for many years, namely until the time of Ordulph, count of Cornwall and of the adjacent land of Devon. Now this count, when one day he came to Lanrihorn and was praying earnestly in the church, beheld the shrine in which the relics of the holy man were placed. And when he had inquired [whose body it was], and had been told by the chaplain of that church that in that shrine were contained the relics of Saint Rumun, with the sole exception of the head, he had it [*i.e.* the shrine] carried to the place where now it rests, that is, into Devon, to the town (*villa*) which is called Tavistoke, where he founded a church and enriched it with great gifts and much land, and there the body of the said count also now rests. In which place, by the merits of Saint Rumon, many benefits of healing are granted to those who come and ask worthily, to the praise and glory of our Lord Jesus Christ, who with the Father and the Holy Ghost liveth and reigneth, God for ever and ever. Amen.

Explicit vita Sancti Rumoni

The festival of the most holy Rumon, the glorious confessor and bishop, is celebrated on the morrow of the Beheading of S. John the Baptist, *i.e.* June 25 [*sic.*].[15]

[15] The scribe has made an odd blunder. The feast of the *obitus* of S. Rumon is Aug. 30, which is, as he says, the day after the feast of the Beheading of S. John Baptist (August 29): June 24 is the feast of the *Nativity* of the Baptist. In a moment of forgetfulness the scribe has confused the two festivals. He has written "the Beheading" and then given the date of the Nativity—At the British Museum is a very interesting document (Harley MS. 3776) described as a *Martilogium*, but really a numbered list of saints honoured in Somerset, Devon and Cornwall. No. 59 in this list (c. 1216) is as follows:

De Sancto Rumone viio Kal. Julii.

In comitatu Deuonie apud Tauestoke iacet sanctus Rumon heremita de hibernia oriundus vbi pontificali infula functus est sed ob amorem Ihesu propriam patriam relinquens in parua britannia in abstinentia magna et virtute vitam consummauit

continued on next page

The Life of S. Rumon which we have now placed before the reader is, with the exception of the last section, which is entirely new, and a few touches added to the first section, copied from the *Vita Ronani*, which was written by a canon of Quimper cathedral in the tenth century,[16] by the same author as the even more famous Life of S. Corentin.[17] It has been printed by the Bollandists in their catalogue of the Latin hagiographical manuscripts in the National Library of Paris (Brussels, 1889, pp. 438-458). There are no traditions about S. Ronan in Brittany to-day except those recorded in this *Vita*.

There can be no reasonable doubt, as I have said before, that the Breton S. Ronan is a historical character. But there can be nothing historical in what is related about him in his Life. It is clearly a collection of Locronan folklore, which the author had ample opportunity of making, for Locronan is quite near Quimper. The incident of the saint being accused of being a werewolf reminds us of the story in Boschet's *Vie du Père Maunoir* (p. 191) of how the same accusation was brought against the famous missioner by a Breton peasant woman. (The neighbourhood of Quimper was infested with wolves down to quite recent times.) The arm cut from the saint's body and restored seems to be intended to refute the claims of some other church to possess one of his arms.[18] The incident of the body carried by the oxen to the place chosen by the saint is a commonplace of Celtic hagiography, and seems ultimately to be derived, as Father Grosjean suggests, from 1 Sam. c. vi. The author knew of the existence of Saint-Renan in Léon, and of the church of S. Renan at Hillion

[16] The story of the three counts must be a reminiscence of a short period in Breton history, between 874 and 890, when the counts of Cornouaille, Rennes and Vannes shared in ruling the country. But the *Vita* cannot have been written then, as M. Calan (*Mélanges Hist.* vol. i, p. 110) contends, since the exodus of the relics of Breton saints in 914 is mentioned.

[17] See Largillière, *Saint Corentin* (Quimper, 1925), pp. 20-22.

[18] This is the suggestion of Latouche, *op. cit.*, p. 93.

---

continued from previous page

cuius corpus apud Tauestoke proprie prope Cornubiam in Anglia preter solutum solum capud modo requiescit.

Now it is evident that the author of this "Martilogium" had seen the *Vita Rumonis*, and probably the identical Gotha manuscript which contains it. He has, first, the saint's name written as if it were a noun of the 3rd declension (*cf.* p. 9). Then he has the same blunder about the date. Finally, the following expressions are copied (with a few extremely small variations) form the *Vita*: "Deuonie apud Tauestoke .... de Hibernia oriundus .... pontificali .... patriam relinquens .... cuius corpus apud Tauestoke prope Cornubiam ... preter solum capud modo requiescit." This may afford a most valuable clue to the *provenance* of the Gotha manuscript.

near Saint-Brieuc. But we should be doing a great injustice to the Celtic saints if we were to estimate their character and work by these picturesque fairy tales invented centuries after their death. Even so great a writer as Ernest Renan does not seem to realize that the stories repeated about his eponym in the middle ages do not give us any true idea of what he was really like: "He was an earth spirit rather than a saint," he says. "In character he was violent and rather capricious."[19]

A circumstance which strikes one in reading the *Vita Ronani* is the unconvincing way the author deals with the history of the relics of the saint during and after their alleged removal from Brittany in the first half of the tenth century. The Breton saints whose bodies were carried for safety's sake into the interior of France during the occupation of the country by the Northmen from 914 to 939 are usually honoured in the places to which their relics were taken. Now there is no cult of S. Ronan in France outside Brittany, and there is not a hint in the Life as to where his body rested during those years. The section describing its return (c. 12) has some remarkable incoherencies. An account of the rebuilding of the "oratory" at Locronan is clumsily interpolated between a statement that the saint's head was returned to Cornouaille and a miracle wrought by his body at Quimper, whither (we are now informed) it had been brought from the oratory. No information is given us as to whether the head was eventually placed with the body, and the *Vita Rumonis* some considerable time afterwards slavishly reproduces the clause in the title of c. 12 in the *Vita Ronani* about the "solius sancti Ronani capitis reversio."

At some time in the middle ages a writer on this side of the Channel, searching for a Life of S. Rumon, read the *Vita Ronani* and adapted it for his purpose. He followed it closely, sometimes reproducing whole sentences word for word, but more often summarizing and abridging the story. He has retained the archaic form of the name of S. Corentin and the unusual form *Confluencia* as a latinization of *Quimper*. But he has left out all the tedious speeches and moral reflections and avoided the pedantry of the original, and confined himself to a brief, sensible and not ill-written (if one may except the too-frequent repetition of the words *sanctus vir*) analysis of its main features. When and by whom was this done?

[19] *Souvenirs d'enfance et de jeunesse*, c. ii.

Scholars judging by Leland's extracts have assumed that it was the work of the monks of Tavistock. If so, it must have been after 1120, for William of Malmesbury states definitely that they had no Life of him then. But an examination of the *Vita Rumonis* does not give the impression that it was written at Tavistock. The *Vita S. Nectani* and the *Vita S. Petroci* of the Gotha manuscript were confessedly written at Hartland and Bodmin respectively, and abound in local references and stories of miracles at the tombs of these two saints. But the brief mention of Tavistock at the beginning and end of the *Vita Rumonis* is strangely vague, and no miracle at the saint's shrine is described.

The reader will remember that Leland inserts the word "Falemutha" in his statement about the translation of the saint's body by Ordulph. Is it possible that the *Vita Rumonis* may have been written at Glasney College, near Penryn? In my studies on S. Kea and S. Meriadoc I have shown that the canons of Glasney (which was, as Mr Henderson said, "the literary centre of Cornwall in the middle ages") were in constant communication with Brittany, and certainly wrote the Lives of Cornish saints who were honoured in Brittany. There was no direct communication between the distant abbey of Tavistock and Brittany. In any case, the *Vita Rumonis* is a fresh example of the literary exchanges between Brittany and other Celtic countries before the Reformation, though as an addition to our knowledge of S. Rumon it is disappointing, with the exception of the story in the last section, which is of the greatest interest and almost certainly true. It was known before the discovery of this Life that Ordulph brought the body of S. Rumon to Tavistock (no gift could be more welcome to a newly-founded monastery in the middle ages than the body of a saint), but none knew where he found it.

In conclusion, it would seem that the *Vita Rumonis* is simply another instance of the expedient, so well-known to students of Celtic hagiography, which consists in the appropriation for a saint who possessed no Life of the Life of some other saint whose name appeared to resemble his.[20] The arguments against S. Rumon being the same as the Breton S. Ronan seem overwhelming. No doubt *Rumon* and *Ronan* are, as I have said, both derived from *Romanus*. But S. Rumon is honoured in Cornwall on a different day from that of the feast of S. Ronan in Brittany, and the existence of a cult of S. Rumon in Brittany alongside

[20] As *e.g.* the *Vita Kyarani* was turned into a *Vita Pirani* (*cf.* Cornish Saints Series, no. 29).

that of S. Ronan looks decisive as to their not being the same person. Yet I do not think that the case against the identification is absolutely proved. The influence of the great Irish monasteries of the post-Patrician period made Irish saints popular in Brittany. It is very unlikely that a real Irish saint had any foundations in Brittany, much less so large a number as those of which Ronan is patron. Some clerk may conceivably have altered the name *Rumon* to Ronan at an early date, in order to make him an Irishman, while in two places the original form accidentally survived. Our Cornish (or Devonian) author does not say, as we should have expected, that Rumon is called Ronan "by the Bretons," but "by the Irish." It is just possible that the existence of a chapel of S. Renan in the Minihy-Saint-Tudual at Tréguier may be not unconnected with the Glastonbury tradition that "S. Rumon was the brother of Tidwal," which is probably the true tradition. Rumon was very likely a companion of the Glastonbury saint Kea, for Romansleigh is near Lankey (anciently Landege) in Devon, and Ruan Lanihorne close to Kea (anciently Landegea) on the Fal.

The Cult of Saint Rumon in Devon

In Devon S. Rumon is the patron of the parish church of Romansleigh. Close by is a holy well of S. Rumon, In Domesday (1086) the parish is called *Liega*, in a charter of 1193 *Lega*, in 1228 it appears as *Reymundesle*. It was been suggested that the dedication to S. Rumon is a late one, due to the influence of the abbey of Tavistock, to whom the parish belonged. But there is no absolute proof of this. There must have been a church at Romansleigh in the eleventh century and before, and no other dedication of the church and holy well is mentioned in any document or tradition. There is a place of the same name in the parish of Tavistock (*Rumonslegh* 1349, *Remmenlegh juxta Tavystoke* 1371, *Romaneslleghe* 1416)[21] The local pronunication of both names is "Rumsley."

In King Ethelred's charter of 981 the dedication of the abbey of Tavistock appears to be to the B.V.M. only (*loco sancte Dei genetrici semperque Virgini Marie dicato*) though this does not necessarily exclude the joint patronage of S. Rumon. The charter of Henry I. in 1114 grants "a fair lasting three days at the

[21] *The Place-names of Devon* (Cambridge, 1931), pp. 220, 391.

feast of Saint Rumon."[22] In 1120 William of Malmesbury saw his tomb at Tavistock. He writes "Rumon is there extolled as a saint, and lies buried as a bishop, decorated with a beautiful shrine, but there are no written documents to confirm the traditions about him. Here, as in many places elsewhere in England, you will find that the desolations caused by continual wars have swept all record of what the saints did, and only their bare names (*nuda nomina*) are known, and sometimes miracles attributed to them."[23] William Worcester tells us that the shrine stood between the choir and the Lady chapel in the abbey church. Mrs Radford says, "Henry de Alneto gave, with the church of Antony, a folding knife to be placed on the altar of the Blessed Rumon."[24] In 1193 the double dedication, both of the monastery and the church, to "Blessed Mary and S. Rumon the Confessor"[25] is mentioned. In 1318, the year of the consecration of the new church, a fraternity of the blessed Saint Rumon, for men and women, at the altar of the blessed Rumon, was founded there by Abbot Robert Champiaux (or Campbell). "The names of its members are interesting, some of them belonged to distinguished families and resided at a distance from the monastery."[26] In 1514 King Henry VIII., "for the love he has to the Virgin Mary and S. Rumon," granted to Richard Banham, abbot of Tavistock, that he and his successors should be spiritual lords of Parliament. On the abbey seal is a half-length figure of a saint in profile, holding a book, no doubt intended for S. Rumon.

[22] The abbey Charter Rolls (13 July 1501) mention the grant of a fair on January 4 and the three days following. Mr J. J. Alexander, however, thinks that the principal feast of S. Rumon at Tavistock was that in August. The Monastery Rental gives S. Rumon's Day as one of the days for paying rents and whenever it is mentioned in the rental it always comes between midsummer and Michaelmas. Twice it is called "S. Rumon in autumn." In 1472 a petition was presented by Mary Glyn to Parliament, praying for justice on the murderers of her husband John, under-steward of the duchy of Cornwall, who was murdered at Higher Wringworthy in Morval on August 29, "on his way to Tavistock Fair." (*Devon and Cornwall Notes and Queries*, 1937, pp. 348-350).

[23] *Gesta Pontificum*, Rolls Series, p. 202.

[24] *Transactions of the Devonshire Association*, 1914.

[25] "Monasterium de Tavistochia, quod in honore beate Marie et Sancti Rumoni confessoris edificatum esse dinoscitur sub eiusdem beate Marie et Sancti Rumoni confessoris tutela . . . . ecclesiam beate Marie et Sancti Rumoni confessoris de Tavistochia" (Oliver, *Monasticon Dioc. Exon.*), p. 95.

[26] *Op. cit.*, note 24, p. 126.

ERRATA

G. H. Doble, *The Saints of Cornwall*, Part Two

p. 1, third line of footnote 10: *for* A. S. Sedna *read* A S. Sedna

p. 22, third line of small type: *for* greiving *read* grieving

p. 28, sixth line above end of small type: *for* were *read* was

p. 31, footnote 14a: *delete* pp. 11–9

p. 34, footnote 1: *for* parfaitment *read* parfaitement

p. 63, third line from foot of text type: *for* Royl *read* Royal

p. 64, eighth line from foot: after *Vita S. Winguaoei* insert (A).

p. 71, footnote 32, second line: *for* for the entrance of the monastery *read* for entrance to the monastery

p. 95, third line from foot: *for* later *read* latter

p. 97, line 15: *delete* full-stop *after* Briec

p. 100, line 6: *for* Roduère *read* Rodière

p. 104, line 25: *for* Yyrel *read* Tyrel

p. 107, line 12: *for* ROSCRADDOCK ln *read* ROSCRADDOCK in

p. 109, first sentence: *for* this parish *read* these parishes

id. footnote 1, line 14: *for* convinved *read* convinced

id. in the verse proverb: *accentuate* mère . . . Genêt . . . à

p. 130, fifth line of small type at foot: *for* p. 9 *read* p. 126

p. 133, fourth line of second paragraph: *for* was been *read* has been

Also Published By
LLANERCH

THE AGE OF THE SAINTS IN THE EARLY CELTIC CHURCH
by Nora Chadwick

THE CELTIC CHRISTIANITY OF CORNWALL
by Thomas Taylor

THE CELTIC SOURCES FOR THE ARTHURIAN LEGEND
by Jon Coe and Simon Young

A WEEK AT THE LIZARD
by C. A. Johns

THE CULDEES OF THE BRITISH ISLANDS
by William Reeves

SYMBOLISM OF THE CELTIC CROSS
by Derek Bryce

SCILLY AND ITS LEGENDS
by H. J. Whitfeld
